CENTERING PRAYER

CENTERING PRAYER

A Contemplative Path to Virtuous Living

P. Gregg Blanton

ORBIS BOOKS
Maryknoll, New York 10545

ORBIS BOOKS
Maryknoll, New York 10545

Fathers and Brothers
MARYKNOLL™

Founded in 1970, Orbis Books endeavors to publish works that enlighten the mind, nourish the spirit, and challenge the conscience. The publishing arm of the Maryknoll Fathers and Brothers, Orbis seeks to explore the global dimensions of the Christian faith and mission, to invite dialogue with diverse cultures and religious traditions, and to serve the cause of reconciliation and peace. The books published reflect the views of their authors and do not represent the official position of the Maryknoll Society. To learn more about Orbis Books, please visit our website at www.orbisbooks.com.

Library of Congress Cataloging-in-Publication Data

Names: Blanton, P. Gregg, author.
Title: Centering prayer : a contemplative path to virtuous living / P. Gregg Blanton.
Description: Maryknoll, New York : Orbis Books, [2021] | Summary: "Examines how the practice of Centering Prayer can shape our character and affect our daily interactions with others"—Provided by publisher.
Identifiers: LCCN 2021005393 (print) | LCCN 2021005394 (ebook) | ISBN 9781626984288 (trade paperback) | ISBN 9781608338917 (epub)
Subjects: LCSH: Contemplation. | Prayer——Christianity. | Virtues. | Spiritual life--Catholic Church.
Classification: LCC BV5091.C7 B55 2021 (print) | LCC BV5091.C7 (ebook) | DDC 248.3/2—dc23
LC record available at https://lccn.loc.gov/2021005393
LC ebook record available at https://lccn.loc.gov/2021005394

To Juliana, Elise, and Ana.
You exemplify virtuous living and
challenge me to be a better person.

CONTENTS

CONTENTS

FOREWORD

Most of us have lived too long in compartments. We were not introduced to faith as an underlying and unifying feature of all existence. Faith was about going to church and holding beliefs that had no connection to experience. In childhood and young adulthood, our education, diversion, and religion were usually divided in accord with the days of the week: Monday through Friday was school, Saturday was fun, and Sunday was church. Later, relationships and marriage seemed to connect sexuality to enjoyment, but both still seemed separate from religion. Our politics did not take religion into account either. Our religion did not link with humor. Each of these remained in its own sealed container. Yet, we know from nature that everything is linked—every flourishing being, every exuberant life, every evolving moment is perfectly joined. The wing of a beetle flutters only because there is a moon in the sky.

No one pointed out in grammar school mathematics that the glorious unity and interactions of numbers reflect the divine order of the universe and of our own souls as well. No one showed us how our belief in the Holy Trinity illustrated our very nature and calling as beings in relationship. Likewise, we took religion literally, so we missed the many splendored powers of metaphor. We thereby did not recognize our own human journey in the life of Jesus, our empowerment to heal the world in the mystery of the Resurrection. We were not taught that the events of "secular" history in our schoolbooks were simultaneously telling us the story of our salvation. We might never have fully grasped that the sacrament of confirmation was not only about graces to be like Christ but also an initiation into the rigors and challenges of adult life and relationships. Likewise, we may not have realized that there are no contradictions between religious teachings and scientific ones. St. Thomas Aquinas says it best: "Every truth, by whomever spoken, is from the Holy Spirit.... A mistake about creation is a mistake about God."

In the pages that follow, P. Gregg Blanton moves us from compartments into a unity-space. Centering Prayer, in this book and in my own experience, automatically pulls together all the apparently disparate elements of our lives. This happens as and because we sit in silence and listen. In fact, any form of prayer is listening more than speaking.

The chapters are simply organized. They fall into three sections as we explore a principle or a way of practicing Centering Prayer. The principle is one that relates to our personal life, for instance, vulnerability in our relationships as it relates to opening to God. Then we see how an activity of Centering Prayer is directly connected to a virtue. In keeping with the main premise of the book, every virtue—spiritual—is linked to a healthy personality quality—psychological. We see that what is laudable in a spiritual life is valuable in our psychic life. Furthermore, in every spiritual practice we are engaging in psychological work; and in all our psychological work, we are engaging in a spiritual practice. We are never only in one dimension; always in both—and there are many beyond. The final part of each chapter presents practical ways to integrate what we have been absorbing in the chapter.

A marvelous characteristic of contemplation is that it enables us to experience the divine in ourselves, providing a pathway to living out the virtues of Jesus in daily life. As this happens, we develop character—what fosters and constitutes psychological health. For instance, when all that matters is how we live Christ's life in the world, we are no longer so triggered by what bruises our ego. We left ego behind when we entered the realm of the sacred in Centering Prayer. This realm is not somewhere up in the sky; it is nothing more or less than bedrock reality. At a talk by Father Keating in San Francisco that I attended several years ago he said many wonderful things, but the one sentence I remember best was: "Reality is another name for God." He never once referred to God as an other. Thomas Merton also taught that God is not "somebody else."

Centering Prayer places special emphasis on *consenting* to God. We are opening to God's presence in our daily lives, a presence aloud and silent all at once. We are recognizing the action of the Holy Spirit in every life event. Such a recognition evokes a yes to a divine design in all that happens. This is what Carl Jung called the "unconditional yes" to what is. Then we discover, that is, uncover, the divine workings of the Spirit, ever-creating a kingdom of justice, peace, and love.

If our central calling is a yes to reality, then Centering Prayer is a portal into co-creating that kingdom. It is not a royal court in a distant sky; it is God's heart as the center and circumference of all that is. To welcome this, our yes is the most appropriate and only efficacious prayer. It is the one uttered by Mary at the Annunciation: "Be it done to me according to your word." It is the one sweated by Jesus in the garden of Gethsemane: "Thy will be done." Becoming yes to all that happens to us lets us hear Jesus knocking on the door to our hearts: "Here I am! I stand at the door and knock. If anyone hears my voice and opens the door, I will come in and eat with that person, and that person with me" (Rev 3:20).

Yet, a full response to God is not a choice. It is divine grace that endows us with the power to say yes without reserve. We can't do it on our own. Neither did Mary; neither did Jesus. Surrender to reality, our unconditional yes, is not only a powerful grace in spirituality. It is a natural endowment of the human psyche that awakens when we let go of our self-centeredness. In fact, I see, especially after reading this book, Centering Prayer as a powerful antidote to self-centeredness. It centers us in God. What we are and what happens is God supping with us, all doors open at last. Let's also notice in the quotation from Revelation: he knocks with sound but he sits in silence—the essence of Centering Prayer.

Here too, we can see that what happens in spiritual practice is one with what makes us whole in all areas of life. Centering Prayer is always combining spiritual progress with psychological development. In spiritual progress, we let God in; part of psychological growth is letting reality in—one and the same. We are always appreciating how wholeness and holiness are linked, inextricably interwoven within us.

This book led me to a wonderfully new sense of prayer. It happened one day as I was turning a page; I don't remember which. I suddenly realized that Centering Prayer is not a technique. Centering Prayer is a way of finding out what prayer really is: listening to the silence of God. And, in that silence there is only one of us.

David Richo
Santa Barbara

ACKNOWLEDGMENTS

There are some special people I want to thank:

Thomas Keating: Thank you for teaching me about Centering Prayer and for believing in my first book project.

Daniel Siegel: Thank you for introducing me to the idea that contemplative practices and character development are connected.

My parents: Thank you, Dad, for showing me that a person's values and beliefs should match how they live. Thank you, Mom, for your constant love.

David Litteral: Thank you for encouraging me in this project and for your enduring friendship for most of my life.

My editor at Orbis Books, Paul McMahon: Thank you for believing in and championing this project. Thank you for your kind and sure hand as this book came into existence. You challenged and helped me grow and change as a thinker and writer. With your meticulous and knowledgeable guidance, you helped shape this into a much better book.

Jordan, my son-in-law: Thank you for the kindness, love, and joy you have brought into my life. You are a constant source of encouragement.

Zoah, my granddaughter: I am so thankful that you have come into the world. You show me that life is full of potential, that we are all fragile, and that love is accessible.

Juliana: Thank you for demonstrating that intelligence and compassion are a great combination. You continue to inspire me. Thanks for your keen perspective on many parts of this book.

Elise: Thank you for showing me that excellence and humility can coexist, and that perseverance and playfulness are compatible. You are such an abiding source of pride for me.

Ana: Thank you for being an abiding source of strength. Your belief in me and this project have made it possible. I have relied upon your feedback every step along the way. Getting to spend my days and life with you make me the luckiest guy in the world. Thank you for your ideas, encouragement, and neck massages (after long hours at the computer). I could not have brought this project to completion without you. I love you.

INTRODUCTION

Going for a walk is a highlight of my day. I am particularly fond of a path near my house that winds through the forest up to the Blue Ridge Parkway. I have a variety of reasons for going on a daily walk, but my main motive is simply to feel more alive.

Perhaps, you are opening up this book because you also want to feel more alive—that is, more spiritually alive. My goal is to support you in this endeavor by setting you on the path of Centering Prayer.

Centering Prayer

I started my practice of Centering Prayer more than ten years ago, and some of my early expectations have been confirmed. For example, I imagined that it would impact my relationship with God, and it has. I correctly assumed that Centering Prayer would include practices such as opening to God, giving my attention to God, waiting on God, listening to God, and receiving God. At that time, these disciplines fit within my understanding of the term *spiritual*.

I discovered many pleasant surprises within my practice of Centering Prayer. I was amazed to find the power of choice, the option of a new identity, and the possibility of healing. I was unprepared to find Centering Prayer to be a place where I would find greater self-knowledge, fuller self-acceptance, and a deeper sense that I was loved by God.

Over time, I encountered other unexpected elements of Centering Prayer. I was surprised to confront personal struggles, unique vulnerabilities, unhappiness, and my own obstacles to closeness with God. In silence, I discovered my tendencies to react by hiding and by getting angry. I did not foresee that Centering Prayer would unearth unwanted thoughts and painful feelings, as well as a host of unrealistic expectations.

Eventually, I revised my concept of both Centering Prayer and the term "spiritual." I have come to understand that every experience of Centering Prayer—wanted or unwanted, good or bad, pleasant or unpleasant—is used by God for our transformation. All of our encounters of slipping in and out of silence, of sensing God's presence and absence, of feeling at rest and in turmoil, are part of God's movement in our lives. Being *spiritual* means being open and receptive to them all.[1]

Thomas Merton tells us, "Contemplation is the highest expression of man's intellectual and spiritual life."[2] Contemplative prayer offers us the opportunity to be fully alive. However, the problem is that we have misconceptions about contemplative prayer. In response to this difficulty, Thomas Keating and his associates developed Centering Prayer as a method for clarifying and simplifying the practice of contemplative prayer.

What are the origins of Centering Prayer? Centering Prayer was developed in the 1970s by three men: Thomas Keating, William Meninger, and Basil Pennington. It is important to note that it was a decade during which spiritual teachers of major Eastern religions were coming to the United States and presenting their unique methods of meditation. Many young people, learning about these other traditions, came to

St. Joseph's Abbey in Spencer, Massachusetts, where Keating was abbot, asking for a Christian method of contemplation. Since such an approach was not available, Keating tasked his monks with creating one. The result was Centering Prayer.[3]

From humble beginnings, Centering Prayer has spread to a network of supporters around the world. Centering Prayer was first offered to retreatants at St. Joseph's Abbey, where Keating clarified his method of Centering Prayer. Through his retreats, writings, and leadership, Keating focused on refining the essentials of the method. Today, the organization that Keating founded to disseminate this practice—that is, Contemplative Outreach—has over 160 chapters in the United States and twenty other countries. Fifty years after the advent of Centering Prayer, with the support and resources of Contemplative Outreach, Centering Prayer groups are active around the world.[4]

Centering Prayer is not something new. Rather, Keating was careful to draw upon a long tradition of Christian contemplative prayer. The roots of Centering Prayer can be traced back to the Desert Fathers and Mothers of the fourth and fifth centuries. For example, Keating, quoting Evagrius Ponticus, observes that prayer is the "laying aside of thoughts."[5]

A sampling of three other important contemplative thinkers indicates Keating's connection to the Christian contemplative tradition. For example, Keating's emphasis on the power of intention reflects the influence of the anonymous author of the fourteenth-century spiritual classic, *The Cloud of Unknowing*, who described prayer as a "naked intent toward God, the desire for him alone," as "enough."[6] Furthermore, Keating's teachings on the effortlessness of Centering Prayer can be traced back to the sixteenth-century saint Teresa of Avila, who compared the ease of contemplative prayer to the simplicity of watering a garden by letting rain fall on it.[7] Finally, Keating adopted the term "centering" from Thomas Merton who wrote, "At the center of our being . . . is a point or spark with the invisible light of heaven."[8]

Even though Keating links Centering Prayer to the historic tradition of Christian contemplative prayer, he also promotes it as a new and distinct method. Keating writes:

> Centering prayer is an effort to renew the teachings of the Christian tradition of contemplative prayer. It is an attempt to present that tradition in an up-to-date form and to put a certain order and method to it.[9]

To advance this goal, Keating sets forth four simple guidelines for Centering Prayer:

1. Choose a sacred word as the symbol of your intention to consent to God's presence and action within.
2. Sit comfortably and with your eyes closed, settle briefly, and silently introduce the sacred word as the symbol of your consent to God's presence and action within.
3. When you become aware of your thoughts (Contemplative Outreach has modified this language to read, "When engaged with your thoughts . . ."), return ever-so-gently to the sacred word.
4. At the end of the prayer period, remain in silence with eyes closed for a couple of minutes.

In this book, we will explore the notion of contemplative prayer by focusing on fifteen of the key practices and principles of Centering Prayer. However, the only way to truly comprehend Centering Prayer is to experience it. A person can learn about contemplative prayer, and a teacher can only point you in the right direction. However, it is up to you to walk and experience the contemplative path.

Centering Prayer and Character

Thomas Keating clearly identifies the purpose of Centering Prayer. He writes, "The only way to judge this prayer is by its long-range fruits: whether in daily life you enjoy great peace, humility, and charity."[10] Here, in his use of the term "fruits," Keating is employing a metaphor used in the New Testament by Paul: "By contrast, the fruit of the Spirit is love, joy, peace, patience, kindness, generosity, faithfulness, gentleness, and self-control" (Gal 5:22–23).

"You may be wondering, "What does character (or do virtues) have to do with Centering Prayer?" This may be the first time that you have explored a connection between the two subjects and considered Centering Prayer as a path to character.

Why have I invited you to travel on this path? I first got the idea from a quote by William James, the father of modern psychology. He asserts: "The faculty of voluntarily bringing back a wandering attention, over and over again, is the very root of . . . character."[11] In this line, James spells out the path to character—that is, voluntarily bringing back a wandering attention, over and over again.

That is exactly what we do in Centering Prayer. In contemplative prayer, we discover that learning to detach from everyday thoughts takes us to a more profound dimension of reality.

And, at this deeper level, our character begins to grow as we adopt the virtues of Jesus. What an amazing realization—that is, that something as ordinary as how we handle our thoughts can take us on a journey toward character.

Centering Prayer and Centered Living

Centering Prayer can move us toward a life of character and virtues, but it is about more. Because I have a counseling practice in which I work with individuals, couples, and families, I am naturally concerned with applying the principles and exercises of Centering Prayer on a very practical level.

I refer to the practical applications of Centering Prayer to daily living as "Centered Living." Consequently, in each chapter, under the heading of Centered Living, we examine relationship skills designed to help you become more loving toward others and toward yourself. For example, in part one, we will investigate what it means to face our fears, manage our emotions, hold onto hope, and express gratitude within the context of relationships. Trustworthiness, being present, letting go of control, and making good choices that benefit others are some of the relationship skills that we will probe in part two. Finally, in part three, we will spell out practical skills such as being responsible, finishing what we start, listening, forgiveness, kindness, and empathy.

We are setting out on a spiritual path of contemplative prayer. One of my goals is to assist you in growing closer to God. However, there is so much more. I hope that you will become more alive in every area of your life—that is, spiritually, emotionally, intellectually, and socially. My hope is that you will not only grow in your ability to receive and respond to

God's love but that you will learn to get along better with others. I also pray that you will flourish in your love and acceptance of yourself.

In this book, I am inviting you to set out on a contemplative path. The end point is "to facilitate the process of inner transformation."[12] As a result, I pray that you will become a person of good character, a person better equipped to love God, others, and self.

Chapter Organization

Each chapter is organized into three sections. The first part of the chapter will explore one particular principle or exercise of Centering Prayer. For example, in the first chapter, we will examine the importance of being vulnerable when we pray. (Since there are fifteen chapters, we will review fifteen practices.) In the second section of the chapter, we explore how a particular activity of Centering Prayer is linked to one particular character trait or virtue; in chapter 1, we consider the virtue of compassion. (By the end of the book, you will have examined fifteen virtues.) The third section of the chapter is devoted to the practical applications of what we have considered earlier in the chapter. This is called "Centered Living." In chapter 1, for example, we review relationship skills, such as being responsive and developing accurate views of others.

Now let us begin our journey and by looking at an essential principle of Centering Prayer—vulnerability.

I

EMOTIONAL VIRTUES

1

COMPASSION

Contemplative prayer leads us into two primary experiences: love and suffering. The first one is to be desired and hoped for—that is, divine love and union. Of course, God's presence and closeness bring us great joy. The second experience is less desirable and can be quite surprising if we are not prepared for it. This is our exposure to and participation in suffering. It may seem strange, but love and suffering are inseparable.

Thomas Keating, the primary architect of Centering Prayer, offers us a way to understand these two sides of contemplative prayer through the analogy of a divine hug. He writes, "God embraces us with both arms.... If you want to be fully embraced by the Lord, you have to accept both arms."[1] One arm brings the happiness of union with God, while the other arm allows suffering.

Centering Prayer and Suffering

When I began my practice of Centering Prayer, I was unprepared for and not quite ready to accept the role that suffering plays in contemplative prayer. You may have felt the same way.

Therefore, the primary purpose of this section is to offer some understanding of suffering. To grasp the meaning of suffering, we must tackle two other topics: vulnerability and healing.

I begin by sharing with you two useful ideas that I have learned about suffering from philosopher Eleonore Stump.[2] First, suffering occurs within the context of longing or yearning for something or someone. When we care deeply about something, we call it "the desire of our heart." Second, we suffer when we are denied our heart's desire. We suffer when we fail to get what we hoped for or are deprived of something we value. If I am longing to spend time with a loved one after a lengthy separation, but an unexpected event prevents our reunion, then I suffer.

Let's apply these ideas about suffering to Centering Prayer. Think about what is of greatest value to you—that is, the love of God. Contemplative prayer offers you your ultimate good, divine union. But something gets in the way and deprives you of what you so desire. When you sit down to be in God's presence but experience his absence, that hurts. This perceived distance from God causes you great suffering.

To comprehend the meaning of our suffering, we must have some understanding of why we feel distant from God when we practice Centering Prayer. It is surely not caused by God's absence or distance from us. No, God is always near to us when we pray. Instead, it occurs because we are distant from God. As Stump observes, "Mutual closeness is necessary for the union desired in love."[3] In other words, God's closeness to us is not enough. We must also feel close to God.

What is it that prevents us from feeling close to God? Or, we could ask the question another way: What causes our suffering? The short answer is that we are alienated or distant from ourselves.[4] There is a division within that causes a perceived separation from God. This internal alienation, or disintegration, occurs when we keep parts of ourselves at arm's length. Certain thoughts and feelings disturb us, so we fight to push them away. One part of us wants to act in a certain way, while another part wants to behave in an opposing manner. In some strange way, we are at war with ourselves.

Suffering is part of our Centering practice because suffering is part of the human condition. When I sit to pray, I can be distant or alienated from myself. Part of me wants to give my attention to God, but other parts of me want to entertain other kinds of thoughts. When I am not distracted by my usual activities, my thoughts can become dismal and disturbing. What do I do now? If I hide from them, I become distant from myself. If I withhold them from God, I become distant from God. That is painful.

Consider this dynamic in the context of human love. I think of my own relationship with my wife, Ana. Feeling close to her is one of the greatest things in the world. However, having this sort of intimacy entails revealing my ideas, desires, and emotions to her. But, what if I am unwilling to be honest with her about my thoughts and feelings? Ana may want to be close to me, but I have sealed the door to closeness through my own self-isolation. Now, I suffer because my own lack of integration is robbing me of my heart's desire—that is, closeness to my wife.

The Two Meanings of Vulnerability

Thomas Keating makes a relevant observation, "Love, whether human or divine, makes you vulnerable."[5] Here, the word *vulnerable* means that we are susceptible to being hurt. Suffering puts us in a position of vulnerability. Love makes us vulnerable because we now desire or need the other person. We desperately want the other to love us, to accept us, to always be there for us, and to think well of us. However, all of these desires create the potential for pain. What if you reject me, find fault with me, or give me the cold shoulder? The scary thought appears, "You might not like me if you really knew me." So what do we do? We are confronted with an unbelievably important choice. We can either hide, pretend, and cover up, or we can become vulnerable with the one we love.

Here, the word *vulnerable* has a different meaning. Now, we are talking about opening up rather than hiding, disclosing instead of concealing. We admit to those parts of ourselves that we think of as shadowy and unlikeable. We share our fears and uncertainties. We acknowledge where we are broken. We confide to the other that there are areas in our lives where we feel fragile and weak.

Being vulnerable in this way means that we are no longer protected. The risks are immense. Now, the other really can hurt us. Now, it appears as if we have opened ourselves to even greater suffering. But there is hope. The hope is that the other— whether human or divine—will take us in their loving arms. And here, in this embrace, instead of pain, we can find healing.

From Suffering to Healing

Without doubt, there will be times in Centering Prayer when it seems that God is distant, and this experience will be painful. But now we know where this suffering originates— that is, in our own lack of integration. Suffering occurs because of our own self-alienation.

However, Centering Prayer offers us a path toward integration. *Integration*, in contrast to separation, is about the combining of various parts. In interior silence, we can have the courage to approach the dark and rejected parts of our personality. We can face the things we have never faced before. We can allow forbidden and forgotten thoughts and memories to arise from our unconscious. We can be completely honest with ourselves. Now, we can admit who we truly are before someone we trust—that is, God.

When we Center, we have the wonderful opportunity of being completely honest with both ourselves and God. Consequently, we begin to find out who we really are. We can stop hiding our face and stop fighting with our unwanted parts. We are free to admit our brokenness. As a result, contemplative prayer becomes a path to integration. As we get closer to ourselves, we begin to experience greater intimacy and union with God. Interior silence becomes the safe place where we can experience the healing of our wounds.

In Centering Prayer, we become attuned to our own suffering, but we also discover a proper response to suffering—compassion. As we Center, we learn how to respond with compassion to our own sense of pain.

The Virtue of Compassion

One of my basic assumptions is that we acquire an education in character as we learn the art of Centering Prayer. As we are attempting to focus our attention on God, a secondary thing happens, that is, the development of character. We are not Centering in order to cultivate character. It just happens. For example, when you were in school, you took math classes in order to develop math skills. However, unbeknownst to you, you were also acquiring important critical thinking skills.

Let us examine how the contemplative experience of suffering is connected to the character trait of compassion. Suffering, which we encounter in Centering Prayer, transfers over and informs our understanding of the virtue of compassion. This association is not a new one. We find Paul communicating this truth to the early Christians in Rome, when he wrote, "We also boast in our sufferings, knowing that suffering produces endurance, and endurance produces character" (Rom 5:3, 4).

Key Elements of Compassion

The first story told by Jesus after issuing his Commandments was a parable about compassion, a parable about the nature of love. Looking at the story of the good Samaritan (Luke 10:30–35), we find three important elements of compassion. First, the good Samaritan drew near to the suffering man. He touched the man's wounds. He picked up the injured man, put the man on his donkey, and took him to an inn. Compassion is about *coming close* to those in pain. Compassion does not allow us to remain aloof, like the other two men in the story— a priest and Levite—who "passed by on the other side."

Second, compassion is an *other-oriented* emotion. The good Samaritan *felt for* the man lying in agony on the side of the road. Motivated by empathy, he responded to the man's needs. The parable tells us that the good Samaritan "took care of him." The good Samaritan's focus was clearly not on himself. Instead, he was oriented toward achieving what was good for the suffering man. The Samaritan was willing to lose both time and money on behalf of this stranger's well-being.

Finally, compassion is about *action*. The good Samaritan didn't just have pity on the injured man on the side of the road. Instead, the Samaritan took action. He bandaged, transported, and contributed money on behalf of the man who was suffering. According to Paul Wadell, "Compassion is the form love takes in the face of suffering."[6] Because of compassion, the good Samaritan attended to the plight of the man in dire need.

The type of compassion exhibited by the good Samaritan was clearly active. He was actively doing all he could to alleviate the wounded man's pain. However, we must remember that compassion sometimes takes a different form. Sometimes, compassion is not able to fix the wounded person. There will be times when we can only sit with the one in pain, offering a listening ear, a reassuring touch, and our company. Compassion is both active and passive.

Suffering and Vulnerability

In considering compassion in the parable of the good Samaritan, we cannot overlook the context—one of suffering. The man on the side of the road had been beaten and left for dead. What a random and senseless act of violence. By no fault of his own, the poor man suffered terrible, and perhaps irreversible, injuries inflicted by the robbers. It was the wounded man's suffering that drew out the good Samaritan's compassion. Without suffering there would have been no compassion.

Jesus's story of suffering and compassion highlights a key characteristic of the human condition—that we are vulnerable. The man traveling from Jerusalem to Jericho was attacked. He was susceptible to and experienced harm at the hands of the robbers. The good Samaritan's compassion was a response to the injured man's vulnerability.

The suffering man's vulnerability put him in a position of dependence. Unable to fend for himself, the suffering man found himself totally reliant upon the good Samaritan. That which he could not provide for himself—medical treatment, transportation, and lodging—was provided by the stranger with compassion. The injured man was at the mercy of and owed his life to the good Samaritan. Compassion is the proper response to suffering, vulnerability, and dependence.

It is easy to read this story and view the injured man as suffering, vulnerable, and dependent, while the good Samaritan can be viewed as strong and self-reliant. But, according to Peter Kreeft, suffering is universal.[7] Everyone is wounded by others. This surely must have been the case for the good Samaritan. He most likely had experienced the hostility and prejudice of the Jews. He knew what it was like to be looked down upon and treated as worthless. He undoubtedly had wounds of his own. The story of the good Samaritan teaches us that it is possible to experience suffering *and* bestow compassion.

However, our tendency is to disassociate or distance ourselves from those who suffer. Alasdair MacIntyre observes our tendency to think of the hurting as not like "ourselves as we have been, sometimes are now and may well be in the future."[8] We try to create two separate worlds: one that is inhabited by "normal" people, who seek social status, efficiency, and riches; the other that is populated by "abnormal" people, those who are despised and handicapped.[9]

This distinction is an illusion. We are all fundamentally the same. We are all vulnerable, wounded, and fragile. Read the story of the good Samaritan again. This time, try seeing everyone in the story as suffering. The man beaten and left to die is the most obvious. But look at the other characters: the robbers, the priest, the Levite, the innkeeper, and finally, the good Samaritan. Every person in the story was vulnerable and suffering, but only one person was compassionate.

Compassion is about giving, while being vulnerable is about receiving. As a compassionate person, the good Samaritan gave generously to the injured man in need of help. But, as a suffering and vulnerable person, the good Samaritan was also dependent, needing to receive care and comfort from others. He had undoubtedly, experienced care from some other compassionate person. Sometimes, however, the other can be your own self. I wonder: Did the good Samaritan have compassion for himself? Even though the story does not tell us, it is probably safe to say that the answer is "yes."

Centered Living

Basil Pennington, one of Keating's co-founders of Centering Prayer, observes that Centering Prayer is "first of all and above all, an interpersonal relationship" with God.[10] Certainly, Centering Prayer is primarily about how we relate with God, but it also has a secondary purpose—how we relate to others. I call this living from the inside out. One of my core assumptions is that the love shared by God with us during Centering Prayer can overflow into our love for others (even if the other is one's self). The action of God during Centering Prayer can be converted into our actions toward others.

How can we apply the lessons we have learned from Centering Prayer and the virtue of compassion to the way we interact with others? First, we can learn to have an accurate view of others. Suffering is fundamental to everyone. We shouldn't be fooled by appearances, masks, and facades. Everyone is wounded.

Second, we can learn to construct a different view of ourselves.[11] We are no different from those who are in obvious pain. We are fellow-sufferers. We are also vulnerable and subject to wounds inflicted by others. Instead of pretending to be unlike those in pain, we can admit our own woundedness. We are dependent. We can open up and receive help and healing at the hands of compassionate people in our own lives.

Third, we can learn to be responsive to the needs of others. Once we see others' pain, we are motivated to do something to alleviate their suffering. Regardless of how we respond—either actively or passively—we are called to draw close to those in pain. We must be willing to focus on their needs and well-being. Compassion calls us to be present.

Conclusion

Love and suffering go together. Kreeft writes, "If you love, you will suffer."[12] Why is that? Because love opens us up and exposes our most vulnerable self. We are wounded by the ones we love, and we wound the ones who love us. We may not have intended to hurt our loved ones and their goal may not have been to inflict harm upon us, but it happens nevertheless. The reality is that love exposes us to pain. At our core, we long for closeness and recognition from others. And, even though love promises us these things, it also heightens our dependence on the ones we love. The other can love us and meet our needs, but that person can also criticize us, judge us, and reject us. Love inherently renders us vulnerable.

Because of our vulnerability, we suffer. How we respond to our own pain and to the pain of others will determine the quality of our relationships. We can't stop suffering, but we can become more skillful in our response.

In this chapter, we have learned that love and suffering are reciprocal. Love makes us vulnerable to suffering. However, suffering provides the opportunity to respond with a specific kind of love—compassion. Compassion is the character trait that offers healing to the pain in our own lives and the lives of those within our circle of love.

2

COURAGE

Where I live in the mountains of western North Carolina, it can get very cold in the winter. When I venture out on a frigid night, I put on several layers of clothes for protection. This only makes sense. Instinctually, we know to protect ourselves. Even at a psychological level, we have developed trusted strategies for guarding ourselves: clinging to familiar ideas, engaging with thoughts, creating noise, and communicating with endless words.

Let us now glimpse into a world that is quite different: the spiritual dimension of contemplative prayer. This existence is characterized by a form of nakedness, that is, a way of being that is not guarded by thoughts and words; a way of being that can be described as silence.

Centering Prayer and Interior Silence

To pray, we must learn to be silent. Thomas Keating observes, "The root of prayer is interior silence."[1] In Centering Prayer, we are cultivating interior silence. What is interior silence? Why is silence so important? How does it evoke such fear?

First, what is interior silence? It is a particular approach to words and thoughts. Interior silence occurs when we go beyond words. It is a letting go of thoughts. What an outrageous practice! Remember, this is the opposite of what we normally do. Haven't we learned to retreat into logical thought, rationalizations, and lengthy explanations for protection?

Centering Prayer invites us into a different relationship with our thoughts; an encounter characterized by letting go. Surprisingly, this letting go of thoughts is not what we might at first expect. It does not include mental activities such as denying, repressing, resisting, reacting to, and wishing the thoughts weren't there. This would take tremendous effort. Silence is a gentle activity. It simply entails becoming aware of the thought and then letting it go.

Interior silence is sometimes equated with trying to make the mind go blank, trying to rid oneself of thoughts. But, this is not the real meaning of silence. Instead, during our time of Centering, we are "slipping in and out of interior silence," as Keating puts it.[2] In other words, we are never completely free of thoughts. A thought comes and we let it go. Another thought appears and we let it go. That is the nature of interior silence.

In fact, in your practice of Centering Prayer, you are actually encouraged to entertain certain thoughts. For example, you might briefly remind yourself that you are present to God. Or, you might gently turn your mind to a sacred word as a means of letting go of a thought. A sacred word is a short word you have chosen, one with only one or two syllables. It may be helpful to select a word that has little personal significance. As you pray, once you notice that you are thinking a thought, you can turn your attention to your chosen word. In momentarily shifting your attention to your sacred word, you let go of the idea that has seized your mind. Once the notion is gone, you can also let go of the sacred word.[3] By reminding yourself that you are in God's presence and by recalling your sacred word you are reducing your thoughts to "the single thought of opening to God."[4] These gentle activities will assist you in the process of going beyond words, of going beyond thoughts, to a place of interior silence.

What awaits us in this place of silence? Why do we go there? According to Keating, the cultivation of interior silence is the most important aspect of our relationship with God.[5] This is such a powerful statement that it behooves us to identify how silence nurtures our relationship with God.

There are important reasons for going to this place of interior silence. First, silence escorts us to the threshold of God's love. Keating notes, "Interior silence is the perfect seed bed for divine love to take root."[6] It is at this place of love that we come to know God. Here, we are not referring to a human kind of knowing, but rather a knowledge that is deeper than words. When we let go of thoughts, we are admitting that we cannot know God with our minds. We can know God only when we go beyond words to a place of love.

Furthermore, silence gives God a chance to communicate with us. When we release thoughts, we can listen to God. But, this is a different kind of listening, for we find ourselves listening to God's silence. In Centering Prayer, we are learning a new language—that is, the language of silence. Keating reminds us to keep in mind that "God's first language is silence."[7]

This language of silence is the language of the Spirit. Interior silence allows the Spirit to pray in us. As scripture says, "That very Spirit bearing witness with our spirit" (Rom 8:16). At this level that is beyond words, God's Spirit is speaking to our spirit. On this plane, there are no words. There is no human faculty for hearing the Spirit or understanding the language of silence. The communication in this spiritual dimension cannot be heard. Here our logical, language-based mind is of no use to us. Now, we can only be open to and receive God.

This description of silence seems idyllic and appealing, but it is only half the story. There is another side to silence. From another angle, interior silence can be scary and frightening. The trip from silence to fear can be a short one. John O'Donohue puts it bluntly, "To the post-modern mind, silence is terror."[8]

Silence and Fear

Why is interior silence so scary? How does it evoke such fear? Let's consider two responses. The first is captured in the sentence by Dallas Willard, "Silence is frightening because it strips us as nothing else does, throwing us into the dark realities of our life. It leaves only us and God."[9] Willard observes that silence renders us naked, stripped of clothing.

We began this chapter with the image of clothing as protection from the cold winter. Of course, we seek refuge from the harsh conditions of life. At some stage, we learned to find shelter within our own thoughts and words. But interior silence, if we choose to go there, throws us out into the cold. Silence leaves us without a shirt on our back. It leaves only us and God.

My second response about silence and fear is grounded in a question raised by Peter Kreeft. He asks, "Why have we destroyed silence in our lives? We are escaping from ourselves (or trying to, since yourself is the only thing other than God that you can never escape from)."[10] Interior silence confronts us with the most terrifying thing in our lives—ourselves.

Why is it so unnerving to confront ourselves? For one thing, without words, we may actually feel the deep hurt inside. It may not be a spectacular, tragic kind of pain. Instead, we may just feel the drabness, the dullness, the ordinariness of our lives. So, where do we turn? We typically seek protection in noise—the noise of music, technology screens, games, projects, and conversations.

When we stop to be with ourselves and God in silence, we discover a universal truth: that we are wounded. Most of the time, we can pretend that everything is fine, that we are whole, and that we have it contained. But, when we remove the noise, our suffering becomes all too real. Unpleasant thoughts intrude, sadness and anxiety grow, painful conversations get replayed in our memory, and the tension in our back becomes even more uncomfortable.

So, what do we often do with uninvited suffering and unwelcome truths about ourselves? We look for a distraction or a diversion—anything other than sitting in silence or facing the truth about ourselves. When silence ushers us into the room of honesty, we must admit our brokenness. Brennan Manning observes that we can't hide it, evade it, or gloss over it.[11]

When we sit in silence with God, we cannot "put on a face." The makeup comes off. Our clothes—our protection—come off. There is no pretending, no making up excuses. In silence, we know that God sees us clearly.

Silence brings us to the threshold of a loving relationship with God, but then we are confronted with what may be the greatest obstacle to prayer—fear. We are tempted to flee. Silence appears to leave us hanging like a sheet in the wind. It seems as if we have no protection from our greatest fears. Silence leaves us alone with only ourselves and God.

So, how do you handle the fear that inevitably awaits you at the doorway to prayer? First, you face your fear. Second, you face God. Finally, you face yourself. Of course, you will be afraid. You will be afraid that silence isn't helping. You will be afraid of unrestrained thoughts. You will be afraid that God won't show up. You will be afraid of just sitting there in the cold alone. Nevertheless, you must continue to sit there in silence. You won't run away in fear. You will continue to show up daily for your practice of Centering. Keating tells us that the only "no-no" in contemplative prayer is not showing up, that is, skipping your daily time of silence with God. Keating adds, "Even if your prayer time seems fraught with noise and you feel like a total failure, just keep doing it."[12]

What ultimately happens when you face your fears of silence? You come to know God and you come to know yourself. And, without knowing it, you become a person of courage. It takes courage to confront your fears. It takes courage to be alone with God. "It takes courage to face up to the process of self-knowledge," says Keating.[13]

Finally, the relationship between silence and fear delivers us at the entrance to character through the virtue of *courage*.

The Virtue of Courage

As a young boy attending Whitney Elementary School, my favorite class was P.E. For me, it was about the fun and excitement of playing some game with a ball of some sort, but somewhere, a school administrator sitting in his office had another idea. That person presumed that P.E. would promote my mental and physical health.

That's the assumption that undergirds this book. That is, by doing one thing—Centering—we will gain an education in something else: character. Here, we are examining the connection between the practice of interior silence and the virtue of courage. What is courage? How does it counteract fear? How does courage serve us?

Handling Fear

Earlier, we observed that fear is a frequent visitor at our altar of prayer. Even here with God, we experience our fear of being vulnerable, of feeling pain, of being wounded. But fear has no borders. It follows us into the other areas of our lives. How do we cope with the fear that so commonly confronts us? With the character trait of courage. *Courage* is "the virtue for handling fear well."[14]

To cope with fear, we must first understand its true nature. Fear detects and prepares us to respond to the threats in our environment. Once a danger is detected, fear prepares our mind, body, and emotions for an effective response. Frequently, fear protects us by moving us away from the scary situation and shielding us from the source of danger. All of this is done for one purpose—to bring us to safety.

Fear and its accompanying tendency to run are part of the human condition. From the very beginning, humans have been described as fearful. When you read the story of Adam and Eve (cf. Gen 2 and 3), it is clear that they faced the ultimate danger: death. Of course they were afraid. God went in search of them, and when God asked, "Where are you?" Adam replied, "I heard the sound of you in the garden, and I was afraid, because I was naked; and I hid myself" (Gen 3:9–10). Fear caused him to distance himself from God.

This story of Adam reveals the problem with fear, that is, there are circumstances where running and hiding are not appropriate. There are times when we must not turn away from the situation that is causing us to fear. Sometimes we must face the danger, the potential suffering, and the difficulty. We must somehow confront the threat to our own good or the well-being of our companions. This is where we need courage.

Courage is neither blind nor emotionless. It sees the danger and hardship; the potential of suffering. It feels the fear. But bravery enables us to meet the threat despite our fear. Courage enables us to confront and even overcome our sense of terror. Even though the fear prepares our body to run, and even though an anxious voice in our head screams "Run away. Hide!" courage enables us to face the danger. We resist the tendency to flee. Courage helps us to handle our fearful state and equips us do the right thing despite our fear.

Examples of Courage

In Deuteronomy, Moses attempts to separate fear from the impulse to flee. Moses is passing leadership on to Joshua, who will lead the Israelites into the land of Canaan. Without a doubt, they will face the fear of battle and they must not run. They must be brave in order to obtain the good things that God has in store for them. Knowing all of this, Moses instructs Joshua, "Be strong and bold; have no fear or dread of them.... Do not fear or be dismayed" (Deut 31:6, 8).

But courage is not intended only for the big battles of life. Instead, bravery is called for in the daily "small" struggles, even though they don't seem that way at the time. Heroism is called for when we honestly admit a mistake. Valor is needed when we offer an opinion that is clearly not sought by people in power. We must be daring to leave one job in pursuit of another. It takes courage to take a stand for people who can't speak for themselves.

When we undertake daily acts of bravery, we unknowingly develop the virtue of courage. After engaging in repeated deeds of valor, we eventually turn into courageous people. We don't even know that we have courage until some big battle occurs. And then, to our surprise, we do the right thing despite our fear. Stanley Hauerwas says, "Like most of the virtues, courage isn't something you try to have; instead, you discover after the fact that you have it."[15]

Centered Living

Centered Living refers to how the actions—both God's and ours—of Centering Prayer are demonstrated in our interactions with others. The courage that we cultivate in Centering Prayer assists us in handling the fears associated with our interpersonal relationships.

It is sad, yet true, that we can see the people in our lives as a source of danger. What if my friends find me no longer useful or fun? What if my acquaintances discover my faults and decide to sever ties? What if my loved ones stop loving me? The prospect of finding myself unwanted, disliked, and alone can be terrifying.

Without courage, fear can wreak havoc in our relationships. This happens when we accept fear's urge to withdraw from others and erect walls of protection. Distance results if we employ less effort, shut down, and reject attempts by others to connect. Gradually, because of fear—the root of most relationship failures[16]—the bond between ourselves and our companions can begin to unravel.

Fear can gradually erode our relationships, so we need courage. Bravery is essential to the health of our friendships.

Courage helps us face the challenges, hardships, and fears that are inherent in relationships. And, because of courage, we can resist the urge to flee. We draw upon courage to do the right thing in the face of fear.

More Examples of Courage

The virtue of courage helps us implement relationship skills that undergird our love for others. For example, it takes strength to listen to the friend who seems too preoccupied to attend to us. It requires courage to take responsibility for our own behavior, even when our companion is unwilling to do the same. And boldness gives us the strength to apologize: "I've been wrong in how I've acted. I know I've been unkind. I hate the pain I've caused you."

Finally, it takes a courageous person to be vulnerable and to disclose to others the fear that causes us to distance ourselves. It requires bravery to admit our fears, despite the uneasiness over appearing weak. Bolstered by courage, one might say: "I know I've been acting distant lately. The reason for that is that I was afraid you might not want to spend time with me. When I was a kid, my older sister often said things like, 'You're no fun to be with,' so that tape sometimes still plays in my head. I know I overreacted when you didn't have time to get together last weekend."

Courage builds over time. We can take bold steps every day of the year. We are not trying to become a brave person. We are simply trying to face our fear, resist the urge to flee, and do the right thing. Nevertheless, at some point in the future, others may comment on our courage.

living in truth — to desire God is to be truthful with ourselves.

3

Virtuous Anger

Regularly, my neighbor's large black dog would escape and find its way into my backyard. I had grown used to this because it happened so frequently, but this one day was different. Looking out of my kitchen window, I saw a heavy black figure under the peach tree. For a brief moment, my thoughts became jumbled and fuzzy. My mind was having difficulty making sense of this experience. Then, my thinking cleared, and I realized that I was looking at a bear.

Centering Prayer and Expectations

This is a simple, yet true story about expectations and what happens when an experience does not fit those expectations. Let's first consider a few questions: What is an expectation? What purpose does it serve? How does it impact our thoughts, emotions, and behavior? How do we deal with it and the anger that so often accompanies it? You may be surprised that Centering Prayer offers valuable insights into these questions.

The Nature of Expectations

First, an expectation is the belief that an experience should go or be a certain way. Do you have expectations when it comes to your practice of Centering Prayer? Of course you do. Your mind makes sure of it. What do you think should happen when you sit down with God? The following have been some of my expectations: Centering should be a relaxing experience; I want to feel God's presence; I ought to be able to keep my mind from wandering; and I should be able to act better as a result of my time of silence.

Why do we have expectations and what is their purpose? According to modern psychology, our mind enlists expectations to help us simplify the world.[1] They bring order to and help us manage the vast amount of information that confronts us. For example, what if, having decided to paint your house, you walk into the paint store with absolutely no idea of what color you want? You will soon feel completely overwhelmed with all of the possibilities and probably leave the store totally confused. So, to simplify the process, you go to the paint store with some idea—or expectation—of the color you want. "I am looking for some shade of gray," you might say to the attendant. By limiting your choices, you have brought some order to the chaos.

The way we search for information is determined by our expectations. You go the paint store looking for some variation of gray. By limiting the possibilities, your mind is helping you to comprehend your world. Roy Baumeister says that expectancies operate like a round hole.[2] If the expectation is a round peg, you don't have to give the situation any further thought. You go the paint store expecting that a salesperson can provide you with a range of gray colors. If the employee at the counter offers you some gray paint samples, all is well.

My example of searching for the right color illustrates two qualities of expectancies. First, they appraise a situation. In other words, does the experience fit your expectation? If the round peg fits the round hole, we keep it. However, if the experience is square, then it won't fit the round hole, so we may toss it out. If the salesperson offers us gray samples, we look at them carefully. However, if the employee asks whether we want to consider green samples, we can quickly offer a response.

The second embedded element of expectations is an emotional reaction. If the event goes as expected, things run smoothly, and we stay calm and collected. However, when the situation violates our expectancies, an alarm goes off inside our brain. Consequently, we may have a strong emotional reaction—typically anger—to the unexpected event. For example, when the salesperson offers you green samples, you might react with a degree of irritation or anger.

Expectations play an important role when we interact with the person at the hardware store, but what about when we enter God's presence in prayer? How do we deal with expectations now? How do we deal with the anger that can be traced back to our beliefs about how things should be? Let's consider two ideas from Centering Prayer.

Letting Go of Expectations

First, we must learn to let go of our expectations. Thomas Keating writes of Centering Prayer, "Try not to have any expectations."[3] And St. John of the Cross states, "Preserve a loving attentiveness to God with no desire to feel or understand any particular thing concerning him."[4]

To let go of expectations is contrary to how the natural mind works. The natural mind wants to control the options and to limit the possibilities. The natural mind divides things into two categories—either it fits or it doesn't fit. Centering Prayer, however, brings us into a dimension where God controls the options. The conversation that happens in silence is limitless. The possibilities are endless, yet we won't even see them if expectations blind us to the unexpected.

The mind uses expectations to simplify the natural world, but the world of prayer is incomprehensible. The possibilities with God cannot be limited to two steel buckets. The options of "*This is the way it ought to be,*" and "*This is not the way it should be,*" are too hard and unbending. As Gerald May observes, "Expectation is brittle and can only be shored up by delusion."[5] Our encounter with God cannot be put into unmalleable categories.

We must let go of expectations and accept all Centering experiences as from God. If I don't feel God's presence, that is okay. If I don't feel relaxed, I can accept that. If I have to bring back a wandering mind a hundred times, what does it really matter? Perhaps God is in my experience of the absence that I feel. Maybe God is allowing the appearance of old memories and tensions for the healing of old wounds. In some way, bringing back a wandering mind may be restoring my soul.

In contemplative prayer, all our experiences become sacred. The story of Jacob's dream at Bethel (cf. Gen 28:10–22) illustrates this point. Jacob was on a trip from Beer-sheba to Haran. When the sun set, he stopped for the night. Thinking that it was going to be a typical night's rest, he found a stone, put it under his head, and went to sleep. (It's not what I would put under my head for a good night's rest.) After having an unexpected dream, Jacob awoke and said, "Surely the Lord is in this place—and I did not know it!" (v. 16). He then took the stone pillow and poured oil on it as a sign of God's presence in that place.

On the surface, Centering Prayer can seem so ordinary, but the deeper happenings are immeasurable. Yes, we do something familiar, just as Jacob did, but the unseen experience is inconceivable. The place where I sit to pray doesn't seem like a particularly special place, but it is. I may not be aware of God's presence, but God is there nonetheless. To my mind, my time of Centering may seem quite mundane. However, it is anything but that. When I let go of expectations, the time with God becomes sacred.

Letting Go of Anger

You will recall that unfulfilled expectations are typically met with an emotional reaction—anger. For example, I sit down to Center, expecting that it will go a certain way. Yet, when my experience of Centering Prayer doesn't fit my expectations, it can feel threatening because it isn't turning out the way I wanted it to. Consequently, I may have a strong reaction of anger.

Anger is sure to follow unmet expectations. Anger is our way of protesting that our time of Centering Prayer isn't going as we thought it should. On the one hand, we can turn our anger at God: "Why should I be sitting here with you? I don't feel your presence." While, on the other hand, we can direct angry criticisms at ourselves: "You're terrible at this. What made you think you could do it?"

The Welcoming Prayer, an offshoot of Centering Prayer, offers us training in how to deal with the anger that inevitably accompanies brittle expectations. The Welcoming Prayer was developed by Mary Mrozowski, one of Keating's closest associates.[6] It is a process that teaches us three important lessons: to focus, to welcome, and to let go.

When we *focus*, we are paying attention to the physical sensations in our body. Cynthia Bourgeault says of focusing,

"If you are angry, see if you can be present to how anger is manifesting itself in you. Is your jaw clenched? Is your stomach in knots?"[7] You are not ignoring or suppressing the anger. Instead, you are simply observing how anger is manifesting in your body.

What are we *welcoming*? The emotion of anger. We don't try to get rid of the anger. Instead, we say, "Welcome, anger." For a while, we move back and forth between the first two steps of the Welcoming Prayer, noticing if the physical sensations of anger are beginning to subside.

Once they do, we are ready to *let go*. We are simply recognizing that the anger is subsiding. We are not ridding ourself of anger once and for all. No, the letting go is only for now. Of course, anger will return again tomorrow or the next day. Mary Mrozowski used a phrase to help her let go of anger: "I let go my desire to change the situation."[8] Letting go of our expectations and accepting the experience, whatever it may be, enables us to deal with, and let go of, the anger.

Centering Prayer has provided us with training in how to deal with anger as an emotion. Here we find ourselves at the doorway of a character trait connected to the behavioral aspects of anger. Let us now explore the virtue associated with anger.

Virtuous Anger

Managing anger is a tricky. Aristotle recognized this when he said, "It is not easy to define how, with whom, and how long one should be angry."[9] Here, our primary focus is on Aristotle's first question of how one should be angry.

There are many questions related to *how*. How should I express my anger? When I am angry, how should I engage with the person that I view as in the wrong? The way I engage with the wrongdoer can be either problematic or restorative. Anger can be expressed appropriately or inappropriately.

When we speak of anger as a virtue, we are referring to an appropriate expression of anger. Virtuous anger falls between the extremes of excessive and deficient expressions of anger. An excessive expression of anger has been called wrath (or aggression), while a deficient expression of anger is termed passivity. Virtuous anger is situated between these two vices. When we describe people who display virtuous anger, we call them *even-tempered*.

How will I engage the person whom I view as being in the wrong?[10] The answer to this question makes clear the distinction between *virtuous* and *vicious* anger. The goal of the viciously angry person is to win at any cost. The aggressive person's aim is to defeat or humiliate the person who was perceived as "in the wrong." Note that the passive person, though, is scared of confrontation and afraid to change the situation. By expressing too little anger, this person acquiesces in the face of wrongdoing.

How will I express my anger? Once again, let's look at the extremes of excessive and deficient expressions of anger, extremes that we call vices. The aggressive person resorts to hard and excessive expressions of anger: insults, blaming, contempt, name-calling, sarcasm, criticism, belligerence, and disgust. In contrast, passive people are afraid of expressing their anger, so, as a result, they fail to communicate the intensity of their anger.

The manner in which virtuously angry people engage with the wrongdoer and articulate their anger, however, is different. Rightful anger motivates us to assertively engage with the perceived wrongdoer in hopes of winning their friendship, understanding, and cooperation. Because of this goal, in dealing with the wrongdoer people with virtuous anger are careful to avoid attacks and insults. Instead, they attempt to explain why and how the actions of the wrongdoer were wrong and unjust.

Centered Living

Keating encourages us to "work the effects of contemplative prayer into daily life."[11] This is what I am calling Centered Living. In this section, we will examine how the lessons we have learned so far in this chapter can help us monitor and manage anger.

Anger is a social emotion that takes place between ourselves and some other person. How can we use anger to nurture, rather than damage, our relationships? When we relate to others, how can we avoid the extremes of excessive and deficient expressions of anger? How can we override reactive responses and avoid inappropriate and destructive impulses

Principles of Virtuous Anger

Let me suggest three principles that can inform our efforts to reside in the middle state of anger, that is, what I have termed even-tempered. These principles are: (1) understanding the physical nature of anger, (2) discerning the meaning of anger, and (3) expressing anger appropriately.

Anger is a bodily emotion. When you react in anger to a perceived threat or danger, your body reacts to the menacing situation by preparing you to fight or flee. A rightful expression of anger requires first taking the time needed to acknowledge the physical signs of anger. Is my jaw clenched? Is my stomach in knots? These can be bodily signs of anger. It is important to slow down and start here—with your body—when it comes to managing anger. Don't immediately rush to express your anger or move too quickly to act. Instead, pause and acknowledge what your body is saying.

Having slowed your body and mind down to consider what is happening, you can then move on to discerning the meaning of your anger by appraising the threatening situation. To access the meaning level of anger, you must ask yourself: Why am I suffering?

There are two fundamental responses to this question. First, the wrongdoing may be real. The other person has intentionally tried to harm you. That person has engaged in improper conduct and has done you an injustice. In such a case, your anger is accurately telling you that your injury has been caused by some aggressive action and/or betrayal of trust.

However, as we attempt to make sense of our anger, we must consider another possible reason for why we are suffering. Here, the observation of Rebecca DeYoung is instructive: "The tendency to get angry, or overly angry, seems rooted in vulnerability and fear."[12] What makes us vulnerable and fearful? Our expectations. For example, we thought someone should have time for us, but they didn't. We desperately wanted someone to understand us, but they were unable to. We craved someone's attention, but they were distracted.

Now, for each of these scenarios, consider the following: what we considered someone's wrongdoing may not have been real, but only perceived. We *thought* someone should have time for us; we desperately *wanted* someone to understand us; we *craved* someone's attention. In responding to us, the other person has not actually acted aggressively or unjustly. Instead, our suffering has arisen from our own expectations, vulnerabilities, and desires. The anger is real, but we must pause and consider its meaning: we have certain expectations or wishes with regard to the other person. A willingness to consider the meaning of our anger helps us admit the true cause of our suffering.

How I express my anger depends on a proper evaluation of the meaning of the anger. Did the person actually harm me, or was the injury rooted in my own expectations? If the meaning of my anger is based on my own need, then I have to express that vulnerability: "I was angry because I wanted you to be there with me." However, if the meaning of the anger is grounded in a real misdeed, I need to directly express my anger: "I was angry because you were trying to scare me. That's not right!"

Conclusion

In light of these three principles, let us conclude by offering four specific suggestions for managing anger:

1. Calm down: Since anger has a physical expression, take time to calm down within. Pause to lower your heart rate and calm yourself.
2. Examine the meaning of your anger. Appropriate management of your anger depends on accurately identifying the cause of your suffering.
3. Express anger when the other person has behaved badly toward you. If you have a history of being passive, this may be difficult. Therefore, drawing upon courage, tell the other person how they engaged in unjust and wrong behavior.
4. If your suffering is due to unrealistic expectations, communicate the vulnerable feelings underlying the anger. This form of expression is gentle and soft rather than hard.

4

Hope

Many years ago, my wife and I moved from our home in South Carolina to Arkansas, where I had accepted a university teaching position. Our first year there was particularly tough, as we were missing friends and family. You can imagine how thrilled we were when my best friend, David, and his wife informed us that they were coming out for a visit. In preparation for their arrival, Ana and I cleaned the house, spruced up the yard, prepared some special desserts, and made plans for local activities. With each passing day, we became progressively more excited.

Centering Prayer and Hope

Centering Prayer focuses upon the appearance of an even greater guest—that is, our Divine Friend. As we Center and quiet our mind, we are preparing for God's presence. We are filled with hope.

Hope is an integral part of Centering Prayer. Speaking of prayer in general, Josef Pieper observes that prayer is "nothing other than the voicing of hope."[1] The same can be said of Centering Prayer. It is purely and simply the expression of hope.

Hope is not an explicit practice within Centering Prayer, but it is implied in many of Thomas Keating's key instructions.

Five Features of Hope

What is hope? Let's explore five features of hope as it is practiced and formed within the context of Centering Prayer: (1) the aspect of journey, (2) its orientation toward the future, (3) its unique relationship to suffering, (4) its effect on presumption, (5) and how it promotes anticipation.

First, hope is related to being on a *journey*. Using this term, Keating describes Centering Prayer as a "journey to divine union."[2] What do we know about traveling? The first things we notice about taking a trip is that it has a beginning point and an end point. We see where we are and imagine where we want to be. Paul captured this idea succinctly: "We hope for what we do not see" (Rom 8:25). Stanley Hauerwas says something similar: "Because we are hopeful creatures, we're able to imagine that the way things are isn't the way things have to be."[3]

Centering Prayer takes us on a hopeful journey. We might begin our spiritual trek with a sense of separation or distance from God. However, the hope within us imagines that things can be different. What if we can have a direct encounter with God? What if we can know God's love and presence? At our deepest level, we recognize that this would be a good destination.

Centering Prayer takes us on an odyssey of love. Our target or goal is intimacy with God. We are oriented toward a loving relationship with Jesus Christ. We know what we want—union with God. We are hopeful that the way things seem isn't the way things have to be. In Centering Prayer, we are expressing our hope for a divine-human kind of love.

Second, hope is *oriented toward the future*. We remember the past, live in the present, but hope for the future. We know currently that we often feel bereft of God's presence in our lives. However, wanting the future to be different, we seek God in Centering Prayer for the future goal of God's presence.

We never know divine union in the present moment. Our mind is unable to experience the truth of God's presence as it is happening. The philosopher Emmanuel Levinas captures this idea by telling us that knowledge is always late.[4] As soon as my conscious mind thinks, "This is it! I am feeling God's presence," I am no longer experiencing God's presence. I have moved out of divine union and have transitioned into my regular conscious dimension. Keating captures the nature of divine union when he says, "You don't know about it until you emerge from it."[5] I can only look in the rearview mirror and see that I *had* a wonderful sense of God's presence. Now, I must set my eyes on the road ahead, hoping again for that moment of intimacy with God.

Hope can be both earthly and eternal. In Centering Prayer, we have an earthly hope of sensing God's closeness, of tasting God's presence. However, this experience is simply a foretaste of an eternal hope. Centering Prayer reminds us of our eternal hope, of seeing God face-to-face. As William Mattison states, "Hope concerns our ultimate destiny."[6]

Third, within the context of Centering Prayer, hope reveals its unique relationship with suffering. Surprisingly, Centering Prayer involves pain. In our journey toward God we will confront a variety of difficulties. There are four distinct challenges I have encountered in Centering Prayer: *physical* sensations of restlessness and agitation have derailed my attention; memories of the past, accompanied by *emotional* hurt, have surfaced while I am seeking God's presence; at times, disturbing thoughts have arisen out of silence, causing me *intellectual* discomfort; and finally, the perception of God's absence has brought me *spiritual* distress.

Daily, as we sit for a period of twenty minutes, we learn that Centering Prayer can be hard and not for the faint of heart. Our goal of being oriented toward God—maintaining an open and receptive attitude to the presence of God—can be challenging. The path of silent prayer can be filled with obstacles, but we face and accept these forms of suffering with hope. Despite disappointments, we don't give up; we persevere. With hope, we return the next day to our time of silent communion with God.

As noted earlier, Keating acknowledges the connection in Centering Prayer between hope and hardship by using the metaphor of a divine embrace.[7] One arm of God represents the suffering we experience during Centering Prayer, while the other arm signifies the joy of union. In Centering Prayer, we encounter challenges and pain, but we are also comforted by the hope of union with God. Intimacy with God may involve something we didn't expect in that it may include suffering. However, there is a place to turn for comfort, and that is hope.

Fourth, through Centering Prayer we discover a hope that is different from *presumption*. Presumption is the failure to recognize the difficulties before us. When we are presumptuous, we assume that Centering Prayer is simply a method for getting what we want, that is, the peace and joy of God's presence. We assume that everything will turn out just as we expected. We falsely believe that the fulfillment of our goals is assured.

Hope and presumption are different. Hope provides me with the encouragement to continue after multiple times of being distracted and carried away by thoughts. Yes, Centering Prayer can be difficult, but hope won't let me give up on my pursuit of God. Of course, I expected to be more focused today when I Centered, and I was longing to feel God's presence, but it didn't go the way I wanted. Still, hope reminds me that something wonderful happened today in prayer, even though it was out of my awareness.

Finally, hope offers an alternative to presumption—*anticipation*. Anticipation does not establish predetermined results for our time of Centering Prayer. We don't presume to know what God will do as a consequence of our prayer. We simply leave the results to God. But, we do anticipate the outcome. We hope that something good will emerge from our time alone with God. Keating addresses this anticipatory feature of hope when he describes Centering Prayer as "a way of putting yourself at God's disposal; it is He who determines the consequences."[8]

The story of Jesus's visit to Martha and Mary's home (cf. Luke 10:38–42) illustrates the difference between presumption and anticipation. In Martha, we see the telltale signs of a prayer tainted with presumption. In her conversation with Jesus, Martha had a clear expectation: "Tell her then to help me" (v. 40). In contrast, Mary simply "sat at the Lord's feet and listened to what he was saying" (v. 39). Nothing else was needed. No effort on her part was required. She was simply sitting close to Jesus. Her wish—that is, just to be with Jesus—was coming true. That was enough.

The voicing of hope echoes the sound of anticipation. Gordon Hempton, an Emmy Award–winning sound recordist who has spent more than twenty-five years recording the beautiful sounds of nature, was once asked to choose his favorite sound in the world. He replied: "The sound of anticipation: the silence

of a sound about to be heard, the space between the notes."⁹
Anticipation is the delight we feel as we listen between competing thoughts for the sound of silence. Anticipation is the
hope we experience as we let go of a thought, return to the sacred word, and wait for God's presence.

The Virtue of Hope

Through Centering Prayer, we acquire an education in character. Lessons we learn about hope in the classroom of contemplative prayer transfer over and become relevant in the
classroom of virtue. Let's now explore the virtue of hope that
emerges from the practice of Centering Prayer.

Hope as a Virtue

The virtue of hope resonates with the hope that is found
within the context of Centering Prayer. First, hope is about
being on a journey. Embedded in the virtue of hope is the assumption that we are moving in a direction. We have a target
or goal upon which we are focused. Hope orients us toward
our end point.

Hope as a virtue does not steer us in just any direction.
Not just any end point will do. Instead, hope is looking for a
"good" destination. For example, one of my goals is a happy
marriage. This goal is a worthy one. The idea that we are seeking something "good" reveals the value-based component of
hope. This feature of hope is what imbues it with emotion. Because our goal is a good one, we feel strongly about it. You
better believe I get upset when my wife and I have veered off
the path of a happy marriage.

Once we have evaluated our goal as a good one, we set out on our course. But, what powers us in pursuit of this goal? It is the emotion of hope. Emotions move us in a direction. We feel strongly about our selected goal, so we are motivated to achieve it. Hope prompts us to take certain actions—or to set off on a certain path—that will most likely bring us to our destination.

Second, hope by its nature is related to the future. We want our future—and that of our loved ones—to be positive. In the future, we hope to wind up in good places with good things. I want my children to be properly prepared for their careers, I want to hike the Camino de Santiago in Spain, and I want to belong to a church that is concerned about social injustice. Because of the virtue of hope, we look forward to and welcome a future that holds favorable prospects.

Possessing earthly hopes is perfectly understandable and appropriate. However, our hopes inevitably run into a stark reality of life: suffering. This brings us to the third aspect of the virtue of hope—it cannot be separated from suffering. Paul makes this link clear, "*Suffering* produces endurance, and endurance produces character, and character produces *hope*" (Rom 5:3, 4).

In the face of suffering, we require hope. Without hope, hardships will surely stop us in our tracks. Hope helps us persist and persevere when the path becomes tough, dark, and seemingly unmanageable. Hope sustains us during our inevitably difficult times.

Fourth, the virtue of hope makes us aware of the dangers of presumption. Hope has its eyes wide open. Unlike presumption, the virtue of hope is alert to and acknowledges the challenges before us. Instead of assuming that everything will turn out just as we expected, hope allows for disappointments along the way. Hope is flexible and permits us to alter our route toward the goal.

Finally, the virtue of hope anticipates. We don't presuppose that everything will turn out as we expected, but we do hope for a good outcome. It allows us to anticipate the future. Of course, there will be setbacks along the way. We can't make demands and expect things to turn out just as we planned. There will undoubtedly be times of waiting. Nevertheless, we can persevere and anticipate the good things to come.

Centered Living

The aim of Centering Prayer is not just to exercise hope two times a day during our periods of solitude and silence. According to Basil Pennington, "The aim is a totally Centered life."[10] A Centered life manifests itself primarily in how we relate to others. The question then becomes: How do I transfer the hope that I exercise in Centering Prayer into my daily interactions with others?

Hope Is About Change

Mark McMinn observes that "hopeful people have a vision for what is possible, a way to change, and a will to change."[11] In our social interactions, hope orients us toward the future. Hope is the process of thinking about how to get our relationships from where they are to where we want them to be. We must consider and determine the best routes for accomplishing our good goals.

Of course, hope recognizes that difficulties are part of all relationships. Hope is the ability to accept that interactions with loved ones and friends may be less than perfect. The voice of hope says, "Problems are natural." Hope acknowledges the fact that relationships contain certain challenges. We don't ignore the problems that are in front of us.

The acceptance of and a desire to change a problem can coexist. The urge to modify a difficulty manifests itself in two ways. First, it reveals itself when we verbalize to another person that we want things to change. We express our longing to make things better: "I want us to get along better." Second, our desire to alter the situation shows up in how we talk about the future. We express our belief in a brighter tomorrow. For example, we may say: "Yes, we are having a problem, but better times lie ahead."

Hope is not only about the *will* to change, but it includes a *way* to change. The method for transforming relationships is *dialogue*, a strategy suggested by John Gottman.[12] Dialogue is hope in action. In a dialogue, you acknowledge the difficulty that you and the other person are facing. In a non-judgmental way, you agree on where you are. Then, through dialogue, you can discuss where you want your relationship to be in the future. You establish good goals for a better tomorrow. Such dialogue includes a mutual desire to accommodate your differences. Hopefully, the two of you can construct a plan that is responsive to both of your needs.

Signs of Hope

Without hope, relationships wither and die. Hope offers us a way out of and through the challenges that we inevitably confront. Hope involves the belief that things can change, that our social interactions can improve. Our responses to the following questions, by helping to determine whether hope is present in our relationships, will reveal the effect of Centering Prayer in our daily life:

- Are you thinking about and expressing goals for the future? (Hope is oriented toward the future.)
- Do you feel passionate about your goals? (Hope shows up as an emotion.)
- Are you discussing possible plans for accomplishing your goals? (Hope manifests itself in thinking and action.)
- Are you acknowledging the difficulties that exist between you and the other person? (Hope is not presumptuous.)
- Are you expressing a bright outlook for your future? (Hope is anticipatory.)
- Are you approaching the other person in a non-judgmental way? (Hope normalizes difficulties and hardships. Hope rejects fault-finding as an acceptable outcome.)
- In addressing the challenges you face with another person, are you offering suggestions and making requests? (Hope offers us a way to the end point.)
- When you talk about "how" to settle differences, are you displaying acceptance and understanding of the other person's perspective? (Hope is about being receptive.)
- Does it matter that things don't turn out the way you originally expected or wanted? (Hope is flexible.)

GRATITUDE

I was eleven years old. It was Christmas morning, and I had just finished opening all of my presents. Under the circumstances, you would have expected me to be the happiest kid alive, but I wasn't. I was miserable and probably making my parents miserable as well.

Here's the problem. Somewhere along the way, I had decided that the greatest thing my parents could get me for Christmas was a BB-gun pistol. Since they hadn't said anything about not getting it, I concluded (or hoped) that they were going to give me the thing I wanted.

I remember going from the first gift to the last. Each time I opened a present, I was expecting that BB-gun pistol. Each time, I was disappointed. When I got to the last gift, it was the right size, so I still held on to hope. But, upon unwrapping it, I saw that it was not the gift that I had dreamed of. Now, I had to admit the obvious—I wasn't getting what I wanted.

This is a story about reactivity. My reactivity was typical. First, it was driven by fear, that is, fear that I wouldn't get what I wanted. Second, it manifested itself in self-protectiveness. I was trying to shield myself from the sad truth that I wasn't going to get the gift I wanted. And finally, it presented itself in a closed form of behavior. I kept rejecting the good gifts that my parents had given me.

Being reactive is not that unusual for a child. But, as adults, we are invited to develop a response that is opposed to reactivity, that is, *receptivity*.

Centering Prayer and Receptivity

Let's begin with some questions to guide the discussion. What is receptivity? What actions are incompatible with a receptive attitude? And finally, what activities are embedded in the action of receiving?

The disposition of receptivity is often overlooked within the context of normal living, but this is not the case within the framework of Centering Prayer. According to Thomas Keating, as we engage in Centering Prayer, receptivity is our primary activity. Keating notes that "to receive God is the chief work in contemplative prayer."[1] Of all the things we do while Centering, this is the most important. Therefore, it behooves us to understand and practice it.

Receiver, Giver, and Gift

Before defining receptivity, we need to address two related topics—the gift and the giver. First, being a receiver means that we are open to receiving a gift. A gift is some benefit or good thing offered to us by another person. In my example above, my parents actually gave me great gifts. The problem is that I was not open to them. I did not see them as good things.

Furthermore, the concept of receptivity implies the presence of a giver. One of the most widely quoted scripture verses is: "For God so loved the world that he *gave*..." (John 3:16). This brief passage reveals something about God—that God is a gift giver. Referring to his Father's generosity, Jesus taught us that God provides us with "good gifts" (Matt 7:11).

Authors of the New Testament often referred to the gifts of God. John wrote, "See what love the Father has *given* us" (1 John 3:1). In one of his letters, Paul spoke about "the *gift* of God's grace" (Eph 3:7), while in another one he noted that "the free *gift* of God is eternal life in Christ Jesus our Lord" (Rom 6:23). Finally, Luke wrote of Peter's instruction, "Receive the *gift* of the Holy Spirit" (Acts 2:38).

Centering Prayer is a direct encounter with the good gifts of God. God's love and presence are gifts. Both a relationship with God and hearing God speak are gifts. The manner in which God's Spirit helps us pray is a gift. Transformation and healing are gifts. Ultimately, all the activities of God during Centering Prayer are gifts. In one place, Keating even refers to contemplation itself as a gift.[2]

So, what does the concept of *receptivity* mean? Being receptive means that we are receivers. We recognize that we are recipients of good gifts. We are beneficiaries, and we acknowledge the source of our gifts. As receivers, we admit that we are not self-sufficient. No, we are receiving good gifts from the Divine. God is our benefactor.

Challenges to Receptivity

Receptivity may sound like an easy practice, but it is not. Keating writes, "Receiving is one of the most difficult kinds of activity there is."[3] Receptivity confronts us with three challenges. Our first problem is that we want to be in control, in charge. However, receptivity reminds us that God is the initiator. John writes, "We loved because he first loved us" (1 John 4:19). God is in charge of the gifts. Our role is to simply to respond.

Another difficulty is that receptivity goes against our inclination to work hard. We think that if we work hard enough, we can take credit for the outcome. "I accomplished this on my own," we like to say. But we cannot achieve the benefits of Centering by our own efforts. Instead, we can simply consent to or receive the gift of contemplation. As Keating says, "The more God does and the less you do, the better the prayer."[4] In another place, he adds, "When you catch yourself trying hard, relax and let go."[5]

Finally, receptivity is challenging, because it goes against our tendency to possess. When we see something we like, our tendency is to grab on as hard as we can. For example, during my own practice of Centering Prayer, if I enter into a moment of great peace, my instinct is to try to hold onto it. Yes, when I experience a sense of God's presence, I am tempted to hang on to it. But, the taste of God is fleeting. I can't contain or control it. It is a gift that is in some ways dissatisfying, because it leaves me hungry, wanting more. As Keating notes, "Trying to hang on to God's presence is like trying to hang on to the air."[6] Being receptive means holding lightly. It means being willing to let go.

A Gentle Activity

Since receptivity suggests an absence of effort, we can make the mistake of assuming that being receptive is about inactivity. But open receptivity is a gentle activity. In fact, it enlists the help of two other attitudes: *waiting* and *attention*.

In my own Centering practice, I am *waiting* for interior silence. I long for it because it is accompanied by God's love, God's presence. But this silence is momentary. Often, I notice the gift of silence only once it is gone, that is, when another noisy thought takes center stage. Then I find myself waiting again for another precious moment of interior silence.

In Centering Prayer, I am waiting on the blessings of silence. With an attitude of expectancy, I wonder what good gifts God will be bestowing upon me during my twenty minutes of Centering Prayer. Is God lavishing love upon me? Is God bestowing upon me grace? Am I receiving the gift of life? Is God giving me the gift of the Holy Spirit? I am waiting for gifts that are incomprehensible. I am waiting for gifts that may be unseen and unfelt, but my relaxed hands are open nevertheless.

A second type of activity embedded in receptivity is *attention*. Keating notes that "contemplative prayer is an incredibly simple kind of attention."[7] The way I practice attention is by focusing. It is about noticing thoughts. I want to catch a thought when it drifts in, robbing me of silence. Then, I shift my attention to my sacred word as a way of letting go of that thought. Now, I simply want to focus on being present to God. Now, my single desire is to attend to one thought—being open to God.

Let us now consider how the contemplative practice of receptivity can put us on the path toward another important character trait—gratitude.

The Virtue of Gratitude

Isn't it amazing how engaging in one activity can unintentionally produce another skill? A good example is how playing the piano improves our time management skills and enhances our listening skills. The same principle applies to Centering Prayer. As we regularly engage in the contemplative practice of receptivity, we are being trained in the virtue of gratitude.

What is gratitude? What strategies help promote the virtue of gratitude? What is the vice associated with *gratitude*?

Defining Gratitude

Gratitude can be described in four ways: recognition of the beneficiary, a process of placing a value on the gift, a movement from being a receiver to becoming a giver, and appreciating the gift of the present moment. First, gratitude is marked by the recognition that we are receivers. Gratitude is about learning to receive and respond properly to gifts.[8] As recipients of gifts, we become thankful for the benefactors in our life.

Gratitude destroys the myth of self-sufficiency and reminds us that we are dependent creatures. We do not give ourselves these gifts. No, we are a beneficiary. The act of receiving a gift requires recognition of the other person—the benefactor. Our companion—whether divine or human—is the source of our gift.

Second, gratitude can also be described as a process of placing a value on the gift. When we are truly grateful, we don't receive the gift as if it is somehow neutral in value or insignificant. Instead, gratitude informs us that the gift is beneficial and desirable—that is, it is a *good* gift. Robert Roberts notes that "gratitude is the perception of good."[9]

Because gratitude imbues the gift with significance, we actually experience an intense emotional reaction in response to the gift. This positive emotion is closely related to the feeling of happiness. However, without the perception that the gift is "good," the receiver misses out on a positive emotional experience.

Next, gratitude moves us from being a receiver to becoming a giver. But, we must remember the order in which this happens. We are receivers *before* becoming givers. Initially, as recipients

of gifts, we experience the joy and thankfulness of having benefactors in our life. Then, gratitude begins to motivate us to bestow kindness on others. We learn to become gift givers. We
move from being a beneficiary to becoming a benefactor.

Finally, gratitude is organized around the good gift that is
happening now. It is about appreciating the gift of the moment.[10] Gratitude is similar to, yet different from, hope. They
are both goodness-oriented, but they are targeted at different
points in time. Hope anticipates the good things that are going
to transpire in the *future*, whereas gratitude focuses on the
good things that are happening in the *present*. Gratitude has to
do with the good gift that is being exchanged now.

Strategies of Gratitude

Robert Emmons and Anjali Mishra identify two strategies that
have proven effective in fostering the virtue of gratitude: *attention* and *remembering*.[11] *Attention* refers to the practice of
noticing and becoming aware of something. In the context of
gratitude, we are talking about concentrating on the good gifts
in our life. Attention requires us to focus. Of course, we could
shift our attention to what is missing, how others have it better
than us, and what is wrong, but gratitude is about bringing
our attention back to goodness.

Remembering refers to the practice of connecting the attention that we are placing on a current gift to attention on
previous gifts. Gratitude is more than a momentary concentra-
tion on the good gift before us. Instead, gratitude evokes memories of previous gifts. Remembering expands our attention.
We don't simply appreciate the gift that we are receiving now.
Rather, we also recall and attend to the gifts bestowed upon us
by the benefactor in the past.

I recently asked my friend David to help me install wood floors in my master bedroom, because I knew he was familiar with the process. As David helped me on this project, my mind drifted back to all of the previous times that he has assisted me on tasks and plans. My mind held a storehouse of memories of all the ways that David has helped and supported me over the years. That is remembering.

Therefore, gratitude rests upon three pillars. One pillar is remembering. We exercise this skill by observing that the benefactor has maintained his gift-giving from the past into the present, as in the case of my friend, David. A second pillar is the continued belief in the benevolence of gift giver. A third pillar is in the ongoing perception of the goodness in the gift. When these three supports are removed, gratitude collapses, and we could say that the person becomes ungrateful.

A Lesson in Ingratitude

Jesus told a parable about workers in the vineyard (cf. Matt 20:1–16) that presents a beautiful lesson in the study of gratitude. The landowner goes out at nine o'clock in the morning to hire laborers for the vineyard. He agrees to pay them a denarius—the usual daily wage at that time for a day laborer. Undoubtedly, soon after being hired, the workers were grateful for the work and income. The landowner made the same deal with laborers at noon, three, and five o'clock. That is, he agreed to pay all of them the same amount—a denarius. At six o'clock, work ended for the day, and the landowner gave each of them what he had promised—a denarius.

By the end of the day, the gratitude of those workers who were hired first had turned to ingratitude. They no longer remembered the gift for which they had been so grateful in the morning. They no longer saw themselves as benefiting from the landowner's actions, but as deprived. Jesus said that "they thought they would receive more" (v. 10). By the end of the day, their perception of the landowner had changed. They no longer viewed the landowner favorably. Instead, "they grumbled against the landowner" (v. 11).

In this parable about gift-giving, we discover that the vice associated with gratitude is *entitlement*.[12] All the telltale signs of entitlement are present in the story. First, there is impatience, wanting things to be different right now. Second, entitlement tells us that the giver of the gifts *owes* us something. "I deserved this," we say. Third, entitlement leads us to grasp and *demand* "what we deserve." In the end, entitlement leaves us with feelings of *disappointment*, *dissatisfaction*, and *resentment*.

Centered Living

Centered Living occurs when we bring the practices of Centering Prayer into our daily lives. When we integrate the contemplative practice of receptivity into our lives, it matures into the virtue of gratitude. Gratitude helps us to interact with others in a more loving way. As Emmons and Mishra state, "Gratitude strengthens and expands social relationships."[13]

How do we remove entitlement, the greatest obstacle to gratitude? And how can we be more grateful in our interactions with others?

Eradicating Entitlement

To be grateful, we must be aware of and resist its vice, entitlement. What does it look like? Entitlement shows itself in four ways: negative attention, false expectations, demands, and hurt feelings.

Entitlement reveals itself in response to the question: What am I paying attention to? Entitlement concentrates on the negative, that is, we notice what's missing and what's not good enough.[14] Unfortunately, we can compare our friends and loved ones with some ideal standard and wonder: "Wouldn't it be nice if you had less of this and more of that?"

Once we have identified what's lacking in the other, entitlement leads us to expectations. An expectation is an assumption that something should happen. We go from thinking, "Wouldn't it be nice if you made me happier?" to thinking, "You ought to make me happy."

Once we buy into false expectations, entitlement begins to shape how we communicate with others. Our expectations become demands; we hear directives and commands coming out of our mouth.

Entitlement ultimately affects the emotional life of the one on the receiving end. That person is experiencing the pressure, demands, and attacks of the entitled person. Consequently, the recipient of negative attention, false expectations, and belligerence feels unwanted, unaccepted, and uncared for.

The attributes of entitlement are on full display in Steve's interactions with his wife, Leslie. Over the past four years, Steve has concluded that the wife of his best friend, Randy, showers better attention on Randy than Leslie does on Steve. Lately, Steve has become tired of what he perceives to be Leslie's ungratefulness and indifference. In fact, he has started accusing her of being "selfish and cold." This has led Steve to make demands of Leslie, "You need to listen to me when I'm talking. I'm not going to keep putting up with the way you treat me."

Steps toward Gratitude

Now that we have uncovered the nature of entitlement, we want to replace it with gratitude. Let me suggest four steps toward this end. The first step requires a *change in focus*. Instead of concentrating on what is lacking, we must be attentive to the good things in the relationship. As opposed to the entitled mind that is on the lookout for mistakes, omissions, and failures, the grateful mind searches for the positive things the other person brings to your life. Are you paying attention to how the other person contributes to your life?

Once we have identified the good things that another person offers—support, companionship, kindness, and so forth—we must release any claim to this gift. This is the second step toward gratitude—*letting go of expectations*. Don't we learn this in Centering Prayer? Being a receiver means that we don't grab, demand, or take the other's gifts for granted. Referring to the gifts given by others, Emmons observes that "we no longer take them *for* granted. We take them *as* granted."[15]

Gratitude—just like entitlement—must be communicated. This is the third step. Gratitude reveals itself in some form of *expression*. Thankfulness—or appreciation—is our response to the person who grants us gifts. Appreciation is something we verbalize. Have you expressed appreciation today for the good gifts that others have offered you?

Finally, gratitude changes us *emotionally*. Findings from psychological studies indicate that grateful people are happier than entitled ones.[16] As a matter of fact, gratitude is closely linked to relationship satisfaction and mental health. Knowing that you are more satisfied and happy, the recipient of your gratitude also develops a brighter view of your relationship.[17] The emotions generated by gratitude are contagious.

Gratitude is at the heart of good relationships. But gratitude does not come naturally. Left to its own devices, our mind has the tendency to be impatient, demanding, and negative. To counteract the vice of entitlement, we must intentionally cultivate the practices of gratitude and receptivity.

II

INTELLECTUAL VIRTUES

6

HUMILITY

Sitting in a lonely prison cell in 1944, Dietrich Bonhoeffer penned the poem, "Who am I?"

> Who am I? This one or the other?
> Am I this one today and tomorrow another?
> Am I both at once?
> Who am I?
> They mock me, these lonely questions of mine.
> Whoever I am, thou knowest me; O God, I am thine!

The question of our human identity—"Who am I?"—is central to our existence. Centering Prayer brings us to the heart of this issue.

Centering Prayer and Identity

Bonhoeffer presents a number of questions: Who am I? Do I have more than one identity? Can we truly know who we are? What role does God play in answering these questions?

Centering Prayer does not shy away from these questions of identity. In fact, questions about self are central to contemplation.

Centering Prayer brings us face-to-face with the reality of our two selves—the false self and the true self.

The False Self

The false self is an identity based in words. We are not born with a false self. Instead, it emerges as we and others form a story about who we are. We end up describing ourselves as having certain physical characteristics, specific roles, distinct customs, and a variety of behaviors.

Pointing to the story of the temptations of Christ, Basil Pennington, a co-architect of Centering Prayer, identifies three key elements of the false self—what we can do, what others think about us, and what we have.[1] With the help of others, in a relatively brief time, we begin to develop an identity based upon these three elements.

Once our false self is created, we spend a lifetime trying to protect it at any cost. We think it will bring us happiness, but it does just the opposite. According to Pennington, the false self is the source of our unhappiness.[2] When you are unhappy, ask yourself: "Is it because I cannot do what I want to do? Is it because I don't have something I want? Or, is it because I am worried about what people think of me?" When we are unhappy, it is typically related to one of these concerns.

You are probably familiar with the famous quote by the philosopher Descartes: "I think, therefore I am." This captures one type of identity—that is, the false self that depends on thoughts of what I do, what I want, and what others think of me. Ultimately, the false self is housed in words and thoughts. As Thomas Keating notes, "The false self is a monumental illusion, a load of habitual thinking."[3]

Centering Prayer offers us freedom from the false self, because our practice of Centering takes us beyond words and thoughts. It delivers us to a place of silence. Keating writes, "Interior silence goes totally contrary to all the inclinations of the false self."[4] As we surrender to God in silence, the false self recedes, and we open up to a new reality.

When we are stripped of words, thoughts, and stories about what we do, what we have, and what others think of us, a second identity can emerge. Within the contemplative tradition, this identity is referred to as the true self.

The True Self

Where is the true self? Roy Baumeister points us in the right direction in stating that "identity is...not inside the person but in a social matrix."[5] We have been misled by the false idea that identity is self-constructed: "I decide who I am." Instead, we find our true self within a relationship with the Divine Other. When we Center, we enter into a conversation with God. The Spirit speaks to our spirit. As we Center, "our spirit is the dwelling place of the Trinity," Keating observes.[6] What a social matrix!

The true self is defined by *where* it is located. It is not situated in our brain as some neuroscientists suggest. It is not found within a world to ourselves. Rather, it is discovered inside a community that we call the Trinity. In silence, we realize that "it is Christ who lives in me" (Gal 2:20). Keating notes that "your true Self is Christ expressing himself in you."[7]

What is the true self? It is a gift of being from God. Keating writes, "This gift of being is our true Self."[8] Centering Prayer is not some self-help method, allowing us to produce our true self. The true self is not something that we can give ourselves.

It is impossible to give an account of the true self. It is beyond words and comprehension. As Bonhoeffer observed, only God is capable of knowing our true self. There is one word that describes the true self though—"prayer." Pennington writes:

> When we leave off all our superficial activity, when we leave behind our thoughts, feelings, our flow of images, and simply settle down to assent wholly to being who we are, we are essentially prayer—response to God.[9]

Two Elements of Identity

Our discussion of identity raises two final thoughts. First, Centering Prayer reminds me of my *dependency*. I rely upon God to know my true self. It is a gift. In silence, I wait upon it. It is something that only God can know and give. There is nothing I can do to create my true self. As Jesus taught, "I am the vine, you are the branches. Those who abide in me and I in them bear much fruit, because apart from me you can do nothing" (John 15:5).

In Centering Prayer, I realize that the work is up to God. I clearly don't possess the ability to create a true self. I am far from self-sufficient. I depend upon God to change me. I must cease from my own efforts, focusing upon my connection with God. As Keating says, "The more God does and the less you do, the better the prayer."[10]

Second, Centering Prayer is an exercise in *self-forgetting*. This means letting go of thoughts about the false self. The false self wants my attention. It wants to occupy my mind. However, my intention is to release thoughts about what I do, what I have, and what others think of me. As I stop reflecting on myself, I have the opportunity of entering into moments of union with God.

The goal of Centering Prayer is to think less about our self. Letting go of thoughts about oneself can be scary. As Keating observes, "When you get close to the edge of self-forgetfulness ... you may experience fear."[11] Addressing both our dependency and self-forgetfulness, Keating writes, "To forget self is the hardest job on earth, but it doesn't come about by trying. Only God can bring our false self to an end."[12]

Our discussion of Centering Prayer and identity leads us to our next topic—the virtue of humility. Here, we find two practices of contemplative prayer—dependency and self-forgetfulness—intersecting at the point of humility. Keating writes, "Humility is the forgetfulness of self."[13]

The Virtue of Humility

Through Centering Prayer, our lives begin to produce the fruits of character. Keating recognizes this when he states, "The only way to judge this prayer is by its long-range fruits: whether in daily life you enjoy greater peace, humility and charity."[14]

Humility has not always been considered an important character trait. Aristotle avoided it. Aquinas excluded it from his famous list of virtues. But St. Bernard of Clairvaux (1090–1153), when asked to name the four cardinal virtues, replied: "Humility, humility, humility, and humility."[15]

Pride

One way to understand a virtue is by contrasting it with something different. The opposite of humility is pride, the greatest of all vices. Jesus's parable of the Pharisee and the tax collector (cf. Luke 18:9–14) reveals the true nature of pride:

He also told this parable to some who trusted in themselves that they were righteous and regarded others with contempt: "Two men went up to the temple to pray, one a Pharisee and the other a tax collector. The Pharisee, standing by himself, was praying thus, 'God, I thank you that I am not like other people: thieves, rogues, adulterers, or even like this tax collector. I fast twice a week; I give a tenth of all my income....'" (vv. 9–12)

Two prominent characteristics of pride appear in this parable. The first sign of pride is an attitude of *superiority*. Jesus is telling his story to people who "regarded others with contempt" (v. 9). The Pharisee says, "I am not like other people" (v. 11). Pride has distorted the Pharisee's view of self to the point that he sees himself as better than others.

The second quality of pride uncovered in Jesus's parable is *self-reliance*. The Pharisee says, "I fast twice a week; I give a tenth of all my income" (v. 12). Pride has distorted his reasoning in another way. Due to twisted thinking, the Pharisee now perceives that he has achieved righteousness on his own. He doesn't need others. Instead, by his own efforts—fasting and tithing—he has acquired his own goodness.

Signs of Humility

What is the intellectual remedy for pride? Humility. Humility provides a correction to both superiority and self-reliance.

First, humility is a virtue of dependence.[16] Unlike the self-sufficient Pharisee, the humble person is totally reliant on God. Jesus referred to his dependence on the Father on several occasions. One of these times Jesus said, "The Son can do nothing on his own, but only what he sees the Father doing" (John 5:19).

Humility is not about self-reliance but about dependence on others. I am humble when I acknowledge that the goods that I possess have come from another. Humility is a recognition that I am part of a community. By myself I can do nothing. My well-being cannot be obtained simply by my own efforts. Instead, my well-being is a product of the good gifts of others.

Humility intersects with the virtue of gratitude. Humble people realize that they are unable to give themselves the gifts of righteousness and union with God. Instead, the humble person is the beneficiary of God's good gifts. Therefore, in response, the humble person acknowledges and give thanks to the benefactor of good gifts.

Second, humility is the virtue of correct assessment.[17] Humility replaces the superiority of pride with an accurate view of self. Paul captures the nature of humility when he writes, "I say to everyone among you not to think of yourself more highly than you ought to think, but to think with sober judgment, each according to the measure of faith that God has assigned" (Rom 12:3). Instead of assuming that we are higher, better, or bigger than others, humility enables us to become "rightsized."[18] In other words, we don't think too much or too little of ourselves. Instead, we take our place as an equal among our community of companions.

Humility alters not only *what* we think *of* ourselves, but *how much* we think *about* ourselves. Humility enables us to see the folly of investing too much time in thoughts of what we are doing, what we have, and how we compare with others. Consequently, turning our minds to greater things, we spend less time thinking about ourselves. The distinction that Peter Kreeft makes is useful: "Humility is thinking less *about* yourself, not thinking less *of* yourself."[19]

Centered Living

We need to move beyond silence and attractive ideas. As Keating says, "Contemplative prayer is a preparation for action."[20] Let us pause then, and consider how the lessons of this chapter can inform our interactions with those in our various circles of life. How can the instructions of humility and self-forgetting strengthen and support our relationships?

In finding practical ways to transfer the teachings of Centering Prayer into our daily lives—Centered Living—let's apply five lessons from this chapter, lessons having to do with pride, self-assessment, dependency, self-forgetfulness, and acceptance.

1. Beware of *pride*. We must begin with an awareness of the dangers of pride. Without this awareness, we will not take the necessary safety measures. As I write this chapter, we are in the midst of the coronavirus pandemic. People started implementing necessary precautions to protect themselves only when they began to take the virus seriously. Similarly, we are more likely to opt for right actions when we acknowledge the deadly nature of the vice of pride. It can be lethal to the life of our relationships.

   Pride reveals itself in a variety of subtle and not-so-subtle ways. Primarily, it shows up as possessiveness. We want to occupy the position of being right, being the best, being dominant. Of course, this mentality fosters the pernicious attitudes of control, competitiveness, and comparison.[21] Wanting to be on top requires warped thinking and twisted narratives. We must continually weave stories about how we are right and others are wrong, how we have it together while others are flawed, and how we succeed and others fail.

Undoubtedly, the interpersonal price of pride is huge. The dominated person often feels inadequate, worthless, and not good enough. The controlled person becomes bitter and resentful. Of course, this person resents being defined in ways that are negative and damaging. The person in the inferior position feels the shame of being seen as defective in the eyes of the other. The dominated person feels the humiliation that comes from being seen as flawed, lacking, and worthless. The result of pride is *disconnection*.

2. Form an accurate *self-assessment*. Do you have an accurate view of yourself? Your reply to this question will determine the course of your life. Thinking that you are above others is a fallacy. It is vital for you not to think too much or too little of yourself. You stand as an equal among your fellow human beings.

3. Adopt a position of *dependency*. Self-reliance is an illusion. In both a natural and a spiritual sense, we can do nothing by ourselves. Our well-being depends on the good gifts of others. Likewise, our companions are equally reliant upon us.

4. Think less about self. It matters where your mind is turned. If it is always oriented toward yourself (e.g., what I do, what I have, what others think of me), your life will be small and lacking. But it is not in our true nature to be self-centered and selfish. Instead, God designed us to be *other-oriented* so that

we could benefit others. Paul writes, "Let each of you look not to your own interests, but to the interests of others" (Phil 2:4).

5. Extend *acceptance* to others. The opposite of control, competition, and comparison is acceptance. Instead of control, acceptance offers freedom to others. We accept their right to make their own choices. Freedom sounds something like this: "Of course you want to do it differently than I do because you and I are separate—two different people. Your choice is not a sign that I have lost control. Instead, it is a sign that we are different and I can accept that."

Acceptance changes our narratives about others. An accepting story portrays others in a positive light. Our companions are not depicted as defective or as villains. Without competition and comparison, there is no need to represent the other person as worse than or less than ourselves. Instead, in an accepting story, the people in our lives are affirmed, and this is the essence of love.

Conclusion

Strangers like it when you treat them as equals. Your friends appreciate it when you express gratitude for the contributions they make to your life. Your children glow when you tell good stories about them. Your partner welcomes the freedom to make his or her own choices. All of these outcomes are the consequences of humility and self-forgetfulness.

TRUST

Recently, I arrived at my local bakery just as the pastries were coming out of the oven. While sitting at the counter I could see Maria, the pastry chef and owner, working back in the kitchen. Maria, just like other pastry chefs, has gone through rigorous and lengthy training, obtaining the necessary expertise. The basic skills she acquired included knowing how to work with weights and measures, food safety and sanitation, the use of baking tools, and decorating skills. And, of course, pastry chefs must be familiar with the key ingredients. In the end, three ingredients go into all pastries: flour, water, and fat.

In this book, you are learning the basics of Centering Prayer, which is a form of contemplative prayer. You may be surprised by all the "how-tos" of Centering, but, in the end, there are three main ingredients that go into Centering Prayer: faith, hope, and love.

Paul recognized the preeminence of these three qualities. In his first letter to the Corinthians, he concludes a chapter with a familiar verse. "And now faith, hope, and love abide, these three; and the greatest of these is love" (1 Cor 13:13). Of the three, Paul explicity refers to love as the greatest. But we should not overlook Paul's inference—that is, that faith and hope are also great.

So, what's so great about faith?

Centering Prayer and Faith

Contemplative prayer starts with faith. A thriving contemplative practice rests on a sturdy foundation of faith. As Thomas Merton writes, "The beginning of contemplation is faith. If there is something essentially sick about your conception of faith you will never be a contemplative."[1] A healthy contemplative prayer life requires a robust faith.

Since contemplative prayer originates with faith, we must build a dependable framework or understanding of faith. Let's explore the two aspects of faith: *knowing* God and *consenting to* God.

Knowing God

Faith is the means by which we come to know God. Thomas Keating writes, "There is no way of knowing God directly in this life except by means of pure faith, which is darkness to all the faculties."[2] Here, we are not using the concept of *knowing* in its usual sense. We typically think that knowing someone occurs through the operations of our mind. However, faith is beyond our thinking, feeling, and self-reflection. We don't come to know God through our emotions, experiences, or thoughts. As Keating observes, "You can't possibly know by means of any human faculty."[3]

We typically equate the notion of knowing someone with the idea of gathering information about that person. For example, when I met my friend Josh, I slowly developed a picture of what he did, what he valued, and who was important to him. Over time, as I got to know him, I fashioned a verbal description of how he interacted with others, what he believed about God, and what rubbed him the wrong way. You might say that I knew a lot about him.

Knowing *about* God is not faith. Knowing God through faith is different. For example, let's imagine that you are a student of American history and you have decided to research the life of John F. Kennedy, the thirty-fifth president of the United States. You may spend countless hours reading books by and about JFK. You search through popular and academic articles, gathering more data. You even have the opportunity to interview relatives, friends, and people who worked with him. At some point, you think, "I really know him." But, do you really?

Compare your type of knowing with the knowing of his son, John F. Kennedy, Jr. You have probably seen those touching photos and videos of "John-John," as a toddler, holding his father's hand and climbing up into his father's lap. He was too young to read anything about his famous father, but he knew his father in an intimate and personal way. He called him Daddy. It was a different kind of knowing.

Faith is not knowing about God but actually knowing God. As Peter Kreeft notes, "The object of faith is not the truths *about* God but the God who *is* Truth."[4] It is a sickly faith that presents only a cheap substitute for knowledge of God—information about God. We study and gather data and form doctrines about God. Then, we feel safe in a faith built upon propositions about God. However, Thomas Aquinas observes, "the primary act of faith is not a proposition but a reality."[5] The reality is God.

A strong faith knows God differently, in a way that is beyond thoughts and words. Such faith is unwilling to reduce God to certain categories and refuses to adopt the descriptions that others make about God. Instead, a vigorous faith accepts the truth that God is beyond our words and imagination. This faith approaches God in silence. This is how we know God in faith. Writing of Centering Prayer, Keating observes that "this prayer is an apprenticeship in letting go of our dependency on thinking in order to know God in interior silence."[6]

Healthy faith acknowledges that we cannot know God with our mind. It is a faith that lets go of propositions and words about God. It is faith that sinks below thinking into interior silence. And, in this spiritual place, we accept that our mental faculties don't bring us into knowledge of God. Instead, it is love—like the love that "John-John" had for his father—that equips us to truly know God. As Keating says, "We cannot know Him with our mind; we can only know Him with our love."[7] Merton expresses it this way: "The act of faith is an act in which the intellect is content to know God by loving Him and accepting His statements about Himself on His own terms."[8]

Consenting to God

A healthy concept of faith also requires *consenting to* God. Consent is about receptivity. What are we receiving? In contemplative prayer, we are opening up to the presence of God. For me, when I consent to God's presence, I remind myself that I am there for no other reason than to be in God's company. When I Center in the morning, I think of God seated there alongside me. I practice God's presence by calling to mind that God is beside me, within me as the sun comes up. Keating writes, "Contemplative prayer is not on the level of thinking. It is consenting with your will to God's Presence in pure faith."[9]

Since God's presence is a gift, we can only consent to—or receive—it. We cannot access God's presence by our own efforts or hold on to it by our own strength. Keating notes that

"Centering prayer is not a way of turning on the presence of God. Rather, it is a way of saying, 'Here I am.'"[10]

Consent is about showing up. Consent expresses the message, "Yes, I am here." Remember, the only "no-no" in Centering Prayer is failing to show up—that is, skipping your time of interior silence.

Faith goes both ways. When we arrive for Centering Prayer, God is already present. God also wants to meet with us. We see this in the story of an important encounter between God and Adam (cf. Genesis 3). It was their regular, daily time for getting together, and God was eagerly waiting on Adam. When Adam failed to appear, God called out to Adam, "Where are you?" (v. 9). We typically think of faith as our pursuit after God: "Are you there for ME?" But this story reveals another truth—God trusts us to be there as well, to show up.

Faith and Heart

Faith is contact with God. Where does this happen? Some suggest that it happens on a spiritual level, while others opine that this connection happens in the heart. According to some scripture scholars, the terms "spirit" and "heart" are interchangeable.[11] (I am using the words that way here.) The author of Proverbs writes, "Trust in the Lord with all your heart" (Prov 3:5), and in the New Testament Paul prays for the Christians in Ephesus that "Christ may dwell in your hearts through faith" (Eph 3:17).

We learn something about our spiritual heart by comparing it to our physical heart. Where is the human heart located? At the center of the human body. Life originates and is organized around the heart. Since faith happens at the center, it is no accident that Keating and his associates decided to call their form of contemplative prayer Centering Prayer.

The heart is where we open to God. Gerald May writes, "All we need to do is consciously choose to trust as much as possible in God's loving presence, and in this trust, open."[12] We receive God in our center, that is, in our heart. We say to God, "Yes, here I am. Come in."

Faith Leads to Trust

Centering Prayer is grounded in faith. This is a faith that knows two things—that God is both good and true.[13] By faith, I come to know God. Faith removes doubt in God's promise to be present. Through Centering Prayer, faith can lead us the virtue of trust.

The Virtue of Trust

Again, our practice of Centering Prayer leads us to the threshold of character. As faith matures, our confidence not only in God, but in others, begins to grow. An orientation opposed to doubt emerges, and this attitude is trust.

The Three Sides of Trust

Like other virtues, trust can be viewed from different angles.[14] The cognitive side of trust is the belief that the other—divine or human—will do something. In Centering Prayer, we gain confidence that God will be present when we orient ourselves toward God. The behavioral facet of trust is the assurance that the other party will *act* in a promised manner—that is, be present. The emotional facet of trust is vulnerability. Trust reminds us that we are not self-sufficient. We depend on God, and we wait for God's presence. This renders us vulnerable.

I remember as a young boy going to a baseball game with a friend. As his mother dropped us off at the park. She promised to pick us up at a certain time. I knew that she was capable of doing something for me that I could not do for myself, that is, drive me home. At that time, I had no reason to doubt that she would fulfill her promise. In addition, I had a sense of vulnerability. I knew she needed to pick us up on time, because the area around the ballpark was considered a high-crime area. Unfortunately, she was late. By the time she arrived, we were sitting alone outside the park. Everyone else had left. Knowing that the area was unsafe, I was understandably afraid. From this experience, I learned that his mother was untrustworthy. As a result, I did not trust her again.

Nevertheless, I am fortunate to have a trustworthy wife. I believe that she is capable of adding good things to my life, and if she doesn't, I can be harmed. That possibility of threat brings with it a sense of vulnerability. My view of her indicates that I believe she is trustworthy. For example, I trust her to keep her promises, to care about my feelings, and to control the impulse to buy that expensive Italian purse that catches her eye. But trust can go both ways. If I prove trustworthy, my wife can also put her trust in me. For example, she expects me to be where I said I would be and to do what I said I would do.

Trust is about relying on someone else, even if the task is difficult for them. Even when I am hard to live with—because I am irritable, sick, or overly sensitive—I trust that my wife will look out for my well-being. A trustworthy person is there for us, even when we are a nuisance or a burden. A trustworthy person has our back, even when it requires a sacrifice on their part.

Trust as a Social Event

Trust is not a solitary endeavor—something that I can create on my own. I can't decide to trust another person regardless of that person's behavior. Trust is not something that happens *within* a person. Instead, trust is a social event. It happens *between* two persons. When we have trust, we have faith *in* someone.

Trust goes both ways. It requires the participation of two parties. If God is the other party, I put my trust *in* God; I have trust in God to be present. But then it changes, and I become the object of God's trust. God puts trust *in* me; God trusts me to show up for our time of conversation and communion.

Centered Living

In this final section, we explore how Centering Prayer and virtue-building affect us on a practical level. How can we apply what we have learned about faith and trust to our inter-actions with others? This practical manifestation of faith and trust in our daily lives is Centered Living.

To emphasize the personal side of trust, I have created a self-inventory—a set of seven questions that will help you identify where trust is evident in your personal relationships. Since I am relying primarily upon psychology here, you will find, after each question, support from psychology for the idea that I have introduced. You will notice that concepts in psychology complement and extend what we have been learning.

1. Do you consider trustworthiness an important inter-personal quality? Modern psychology posits that there

is no trait more important to relationships than trustworthiness. John Gottman has concluded, "The most widely desired characteristic of a potential partner was that the person be trustworthy."[15]

2. Would others say that you show up for them when they need you, or just when it's convenient? Psychologists have settled on one question that best captures the meaning of trust—"Are you there for me?"[16] Other important interpersonal concerns are embedded in this query: Are you available when I need you? Will you respond when I make myself vulnerable? Will you show interest when I tell you something very personal?

3. Do others benefit from your presence? The field of psychology connects trust with the concept of presence.[17] Of course, to be present you have to show up. But how do you make your presence known? Are you standoffish or offensive? Are you cold or angry? Presence is about moving toward someone in an accepting and attentive way. Presence is about "being open, now, to whatever is."[18]

4. Do you believe that trust impacts people's health? The science of trust draws a direct link between trust and heart health. Gottman's research reveals that the wife's trust in her husband lowers, not only her own blood pressure, but his as well.[19] Trust is actually good for your heart.

5. Would other people say that you frequently answer "yes" to their requests for assistance? Responding with a "yes" indicates receptivity, and "trust is a state of receptivity."[20] We are being receptive—and thus we are building trust—when we say things like: "Yes, I can stop and listen to what you're saying." "Yes, I can

carve out time for us to be together." "Yes, I understand your point of view." The opposite of receptivity is reactivity. Reactivity demonstrates itself in the word "No": "No, I can't listen to you right now." "No, I don't have time to spend with you this week." "No, I disagree with you." Gottman refers to people who say "yes" more often than "no" as masters of relationships.[21] Would you like that title?

6. Do you make yourself vulnerable to others? Trust is about vulnerability.[22] Do you take a chance on another person being safe and open up to them? Do you ask others for help? Do you tell others that you need them? When you show others that you depend upon them, you are being vulnerable.

7. Do you work with others on joint projects? Modern psychology employs the word *resonance* to capture the idea of working together in harmony.[23] Do you participate with others to accomplish some worthy goal? When you demonstrate that you are depending on others and that they can count on you to finish the project, that is resonance.

Conclusion

This chapter has been a song about faith and trust. The voices of contemplatives, philosophers, and psychologists have blended together in harmony. Now let us consider again the question raised at the outset of this chapter: What's so great about faith? I hope that the thoughts presented here have helped shed light on the answer to that question.

8

ATTENTIVENESS

It was getting dark and we were still out in the forest. A friend of mine and I had taken our kids on a hike, and we had lost track of time. Now we realized we had only a brief amount of daylight remaining. Being dusk, it was difficult to see, so we were being particularly attentive to protruding roots and rocks along the path. Suddenly we caught sight of something moving on the ground, off to the side. We were instantly startled, and then we realized that it was a shiny green snake. After admiring it for a few minutes, we turned our attention back to the trail and continued heading home.

Centering Prayer and Attention

Attention is necessary when we are hiking, but it holds even greater importance when we embark on Centering Prayer. Attention—not talking—is at the heart of our practice. Richard Foster notes that "contemplative prayer is a loving attentiveness to God. In contemplative prayer talk recedes into the background."[1] As Paul Wadell points out, "To pray is to give our attention to God."[2]

One of the gentle activities of Centering Prayer is attention. It is not easy, but it is simple. Thomas Keating writes,

"Contemplative prayer is an incredibly simple kind of attention."[3] Let us now consider this "simple kind of attention."

Two Objects of Attention

Centering Prayer is "simple" because there are only two objects of our attention—God and thoughts. Of course, our plan is to focus on God. As Keating notes, "Our attention is simply given to the presence of Jesus."[4] But, before we know it, our attention gets captured by some shiny and active thought.

At this point, we discover the dynamic nature of attention. It is always changing and active. If we think the goal of Centering Prayer is the absence of thoughts, we will be sorely disappointed and frustrated with our practice. Instead, Centering Prayer is an ongoing process of paying attention to God's presence, noticing that our attention has wandered, and then bringing our attention back to our original purpose.

Pulled and Guided Attention

It is useful to think of attention as being either pulled or guided.[5] *Pulled* means that some thought has yanked our attention away from the thing that we intended to concentrate on. In a way, we have been acted upon by the thought. For example, in the story that opened this chapter, our intention was to focus on the trail, but something unexpected captured our attention. We couldn't help but get distracted.

Getting distracted is not a bad thing. The word *bad* indicates that you have done something unacceptable. It is not wrong, but normal, to get distracted when you practice Centering Prayer. Daniel Siegel states that "wandering is just what the mind does—no need to judge or be angry at the wandering, or at yourself. If your mind wanders and attention strays, it means one thing: You are human."[6]

It is normal for your attention to wander. It is not unusual to get sidetracked many times during your Centering Prayer. In fact, it is actually a good thing to get distracted, because it gives you another opportunity to offer your attention to God.

Only two types of distractions are problematic. The first is when we get caught up in a thought that we are unwilling to release. For example, while praying, your thoughts start focusing on your work, and you don't want to let go of them. The second problematic distraction is when the diversion is so great that we quit praying in order to serve the thought that has caught our attention. For example, while I'm Centering, the idea for my next chapter seems so good that I immediately want to go to my office and start working on my computer. Keating notes, "There are no distractions in contemplative prayer unless you really want to be distracted or if you get up and leave."[7]

The key question is: What do we do when we notice that something has captured our attention? The next step in Centering Prayer is to let go of or detach from the thought. Keating instructs us, "Centering Prayer as a discipline is designed to withdraw our attention from the ordinary flow of our thoughts."[8]

This is where *guided* attention comes into play, and our role in contemplative prayer becomes important. Here, we move our attention away from the thought that pulled us away from our original target and guide our focus back to the initial object of attention.

This is not so hard if breathing is the target of your attention, but what if you want to focus on God's presence? God is not an object. God's presence is beyond our comprehension.

What are we guiding our attention back to if not back to God? In Centering Prayer, we are shining the light back on our intention. Our intention is to be open. So, in a way, we are bringing our attention back to ourselves. Am I making myself present to God? Am I being open to God?

Keating offers two suggestions for guiding our attention back to God.[9] One way is to let go of the thought that pulled our attention away from openness to God in the first place. The second strategy is more explicit. It is simply to return to and use our sacred word, something that we discuss later in chapter 13.

Focal and Non-Focal Attention

Contemplative prayer offers us an education of the mind. Many people view their mind or their thoughts as something that they can control. "I have this thought because I have chosen it," they claim. To them, it seems as if they are choosing to focus their attention on one thought versus another. However, in Centering Prayer, we discover something different, that is, that thoughts can also appear out of the dark, on their own. Somehow, a thought captures our attention without even getting our permission.

To help shed light on what actually happens, consider this example. I have decided to write a chapter on a particular topic. I am paying attention to and thinking about my notes on the subject. I am aware of these thoughts and know that I am aware of these thoughts. This is focal attention.[10]

However, other hidden mental processes are taking place at the same time: my body is working to maintain my balance in my chair; without realizing it, I might shift my posture to get more comfortable; at some level I may start getting restless due to hunger and abruptly get up and go to the kitchen for something to eat. I was not consciously aware of the thought, "I'm hungry. I need to fix lunch," but I was thinking it nevertheless. It was outside of my conscious awareness. This is nonfocal attention.

This same type of thing happens in Centering Prayer. My original intention is to be open to God's presence. I am conscious of this thought. Then, without my awareness, an idea pulls my attention away from my initial focus. All of a sudden, I start thinking about a project that I need to work on later today. Then, at some point, my thoughts move from outside of my awareness into my awareness. Then, and only then, do I have the opportunity to use my sacred word as a method to guide my attention back to my original intention of being open to God.

As we practice guiding our attention back to God's presence, we are becoming better thinkers. Directing and redirecting our attention back to our intention changes the way we think. As we focus and gently refocus our attention, our thinking processes are being altered. We are cultivating the intellectual character trait of attentiveness.

The Virtue of Attentiveness

William James, often referred to as the father of American psychology, notedly wrote, "The faculty of bringing back a wandering attention, over and over, is the very root of ... character."[11] In this line from James, there is a link between contemplative prayer and character. That is one of the main points of this book—that contemplative prayer is a path to building character. Here, we are examining the connection between the Centering practice of attention and the virtue of attentiveness.

We have learned how easy it is to get distracted. We can readily get off-track and lost. However, attention is the intellectual virtue that keeps us on-track. Jason Baehr outlines four characteristics of the virtue of attentiveness.[12] First, attentiveness is about being *present*. Attentive people are absorbed and invested in the current experience. When their thoughts wander into the past or future, they guide their attention back to the task at hand.

We saw this first element in contemplative prayer. In writing of Centering Prayer, Keating states, "This method of prayer is designed to bring you into the present."[13] If I begin thinking about an idea for this book while I am Centering, I can return to the present by using my sacred word as shorthand for: "I will go to my study later to write."

This first element of attentiveness is captured in a parable about the servants told by Jesus:

> "Be dressed for action and have your lamps lit; be like those who are waiting for their master to return from the wedding banquet, so that they may open the door for him as soon as he comes and knocks. Blessed are those slaves whom the master finds alert when he comes; truly I tell you, he will fasten his belt and have them sit down to eat, and he will come and serve them." (Luke 12:35–37)

This scripture passage describes servants who were present-oriented. Yes, they may have become distracted after their master left. However, by the time he returns, they are waiting, ready, tuned in. Notice how they open the door "as soon as he comes." An element of being attentive is being in the present.

Second, attentiveness is about being *quick to notice*. Attentive people are aware of details that others are likely to miss. We see how this skill develops within the context of contemplative prayer. When our attention is pulled away by a distracting thought, there is a point at which we observe it. Sometimes, it may take a few moments for the unanticipated thought to enter our awareness, but at other times, we may notice it more quickly.

Mark tells a story about Jesus that illustrates this second characteristic of attentiveness:

> He sat down opposite the treasury, and watched the crowd putting money into the treasury. Many rich people put in large sums. A poor widow came and put in two small copper coins, which are worth a penny. (Mark 12:41–42)

This story illustrates the attention that Jesus gives to this woman. He is tuned in to the fine details. The situation is crowded and busy. People are elbowing each other and lots of money is being tossed into a collection container. But, amid this chaos, Jesus is not distracted from the poor widow. The writer notes that Jesus observed "two small copper coins." Jesus was quick to notice.

Third, attentiveness is about staying *alert and focused*. This is the opposite of becoming dull, checking out, and daydreaming. In Centering Prayer, we cannot become passive. If we do, our mind becomes overwhelmed with one thought after another. Instead, we must be alert to each new thought, catching it, letting go, and guiding our attention back to God.

Staying alert and focused refers to how we process information. We cannot focus on everything, so being attentive helps us to filter out unimportant data. Attention is selective, helping us concentrate on one thing. We see this quality in both of the previous quotes from scripture. The servants were paying attention to one thing—their master; Jesus was focused on one thing—the poor widow.

Finally, attentiveness manifests itself in one primary activity —*listening*. Attentive people are good listeners, and good listeners are attentive.

This quality is captured in a narrative told by Luke about Jesus's visit with Mary and Martha. Referring to Martha, Luke writes:

> She had a sister named Mary, who sat at the Lord's feet and *listened* to what he was saying. But Martha was distracted by her many tasks; so she came to him and asked, "Lord, do you not care that my sister has left me to do all the work by myself? Tell her then to help me." But the Lord answered her, "Martha, Martha, you are worried and distracted by many things; there is need of only one thing. Mary has chosen the better part, which will not be taken away from her." (Luke 10:39–42)

Luke draws a sharp contrast between Mary and Martha. Martha is described as "distracted," while Mary is portrayed as "listening." We have learned that being distracted is normal. But, in Martha's case, she chose to maintain her focus on all the work that seemed so necessary. Perhaps Mary had also become distracted by something. But, because she was attentive, Mary guided her attention back to Jesus. And, consequently, she was able to listen.

Being present-oriented, quick to notice, alert, and listening are derivatives of attentiveness, but does attention depend on anything? The answer is "*Yes. Curiosity.*"[14] Curiosity *gets* us on-track, while attentiveness *keeps* us on-track. Curious people are not satisfied with a shallow understanding of something. They want to probe further, dig deeper. They are not passive, but active. The curious person is the one who says, "I must see it for myself." Albert Einstein once said, "I have no special talents. I am only passionately curious."[15]

Centered Living

In this section, we will explore how the virtue of attentiveness and the Centering practice of attention impact how we relate to the people in our life. Keating often tells us that the exercises of Centering Prayer will affect how we interact with others.[16]

The Power of Attention

What is the greatest thing you can give a friend, a loved one, a stranger? The answer is *attention*. According to Sue Johnson, "The greatest gift . . . a lover has to give a lover—is emotionally attuned attention and timely responsiveness."[17] With a similar endorsement of attention, Simone Weil says that attention is "almost a miracle; it is a miracle."[18]

Mysteriously, the attention we receive from others plays a critical role in constructing our identity. Paul Wadell contends that loving attention is what shapes us.[19] It is the thing that makes us into the person we are. Attention, in some miraculous way, gifts us with our sense of self. As Rowan Williams once claimed, "I'm a person because I am spoken to, I'm attended to, and I'm spoken and attended and loved into actual existence."[20]

Without attention, terrible things begin to happen to us. We begin to feel invisible. If we go unnoticed and unseen for some time, our sense of self begins to fade. There is an example of this in Mary Gordon's novel, *The Company of Women*. One of the characters is a woman named Muriel. This is how Muriel sees her life: "I wait for a face to meet my face; I wait for a singular gaze, the gaze of permanent choosing, the gaze of absolute preferment. This I've always waited for and never found, have hungered for and never tasted."[21] Simone Weil also writes on the topic of being seen: "The love of neighbor involves knowing how to look at him in a certain way. This way of looking is first of all attention."[22] She adds, "Those who are unhappy have no need for anything in this world but people capable of giving them their attention."[23]

Attention in Relationships

Let's revisit the four characteristics of attentiveness within the context of relationships. First, an attentive person is *present*. When we are present, we are focused on the other person at that moment. We contend against our tendency to get distracted. We know that it is easy for our mind to wander into the past or future. Attention helps us be here, in the present.

Second, an attentive person *notices the fine details*. You catch it when your friend alters the tone in her voice. You are aware when she pauses, wanting to make sure that you are listening. You notice it when his body slumps from discouragement and when he leans toward you for support. Instead of interrupting or changing the subject, you notice that she wants to say more about the subject.

Next, an attentive person remains *alert and focused* rather than bored, dull, and disinterested. What a gift it is when you make your spouse or child the center of your attention. When they see that you are engaged and focused on them, they begin to feel cared for. Noticing that you have closed your laptop to listen, they are assured that they matter to you. As you stay calm and sustain your loving attention on them, they begin to actually feel important. Receiving this kind of attention can be transformative.

Finally, an attentive person truly *listens*. Sure, you might get distracted when you are talking to a co-worker or neighbor, but you are quick to notice that your mind has wandered, and you refocus your mind. You try not only to hear their words but to understand the meaning behind their words. You respond in a way that shows that you accept and value the messages that they are sending. I like how Stephen Post and Jill Neimark put it: "Listening is marked by a profound and quiet attentiveness that is the epitome of love."[24]

According to Daniel Siegel, curiosity is the key to paying attention.[25] Without curiosity, we can fall into the trap of thinking that we know what the other person thinks, how they feel about something, and even what they are going to say. Without curiosity, we stop paying attention and stop learning.

In contrast, curiosity pushes us to wonder, ponder, and ask why.[26] Curiosity causes us to prod for a deeper understanding of others. Curiosity recognizes the mystery of our companions. There are things that we will never understand about them. And that is probably because they are so remarkably unlike us. With curious attention, we can open ourselves to their differentness, their otherness. We can maintain a relentless curiosity and attentiveness. We can continue to listen, continue to be present, and continue to dig deeper into the mystery of who they truly are.

OPEN-MINDEDNESS

It was my first trip to Spain. We were in our second year of marriage, and Ana was taking me to Spain in order to meet her relatives. It became readily apparent to me that all her family members spoke only Spanish, no English. I was scared.

There was only one way to access all of the possibilities of being in Spain and of getting to know Ana's family—I had to be open to learning a new language. I quickly discovered that an essential requirement for learning Spanish was to let go of English.

Reflecting on that trip to Spain, I realize that it was a turning point for me. It truly changed my worldview. The act of letting go of English has opened a door to some of the best relationships and most memorable experiences of my life.

Centering Prayer and Opening

Centering Prayer starts with openness. This is the place from which we begin. Thomas Keating writes, "Prayer is opening to God."[1] He adds that "the fundamental disposition of centering prayer is opening to God."[2] What does it mean to be open? How do we become more open? What are the results? These are the questions that we will explore in this section.

Two Types of Opening

Centering Prayer focuses on two relationships: one with God and the other with our thoughts, and we must be open with both. What does it mean to be open with thoughts? To answer this question, we turn to Keating's basic principles or guidelines for handling thoughts during prayer: "Resist no thought; hang on to no thought; react emotionally to no thought."[3] These three principles reveal the character of openness. For our purposes here, let us look more closely at the first two principles.

The first principle is to *resist no thought*. Resisting no thought requires a vital activity: receptivity.[4] When we are open to thoughts, we receive them. This is the opposite of avoiding, suppressing, and rejecting thoughts. When we are open to thoughts, we accept them. We judge neither the thoughts nor ourselves for having them. Being open means that we receive thoughts as they *are* as opposed to how we might wish them to be.

The second principle—*hang on to no thought*—is about letting go. When we receive a thought, we let it go. Letting go is one of the core disciplines of contemplative prayer. Keating notes, "Centering prayer is an exercise in letting go. That is all it is. It lays aside every thought."[5]

It is important to remember that letting go of thoughts is a manifestation of openness. These two practices are not opposed to one another. If we forget their relationship, then we make the mistake of treating thoughts as if they are problems. We falsely assume that the goal of prayer is a blank mind. But our objective is not to quit thinking. Instead, we want to be open to thoughts, because they are a normal part of the prayer process. We simply want to avoid getting attached to them. This is the nature of letting go.

In Centering Prayer, our goal is opening to God. And, opening to God requires going beyond thoughts. Thoughts are not bad; they just interfere with our having the kind of relationship with God that is possible. Thoughts can block our awareness of a totally new dimension of reality—God's presence.

Opening to a New Reality

Centering Prayer reveals the amazing truth that we live in two realities simultaneously. As we pray, we experience ordinary thoughts about work, relationships, problems, and so forth. At this conscious plane of thinking, we entertain old ways of seeing ourselves and the world around us. However, there is another level—the dimension of the spirit.

Keating informs us that Centering Prayer "opens our awareness to the spiritual level of our being."[6] Our ordinary way of thinking limits us to a superficial view of the world—that is, the way we have learned to think about it and know it to be. However, by letting go of thoughts, we are able to enter a profound level of existence where we are open to God.

Opening is about moving from the first reality to the second. It is about moving from conscious thought to a deeper, unconscious plane. It is about moving from a reality that we know to one that we cannot comprehend with our human faculties. As Keating suggests, "If you turn off your ordinary thinking...you open yourself to a new world of reality."[7]

In the story with which I began this chapter, you will recall that I discovered how essential it was to let go of English. There is nothing bad about the English language. However, I needed to let go of it in order to learn Spanish. It was only by letting go of English that a whole new world opened up to me.

Opening the Door

A verse in the Book of Revelation contains important lessons about openness: "Listen! I am standing at the door, knocking; if you hear my voice and *open* the door, I will come in to you and eat with you, and you with me" (Rev 3:20).

The first lesson is that something stands between the guest and the occupant—a door. The door itself is not bad. Instead, it is simply a barrier between the person outside and the person inside. In the same manner, the thoughts that we encounter during Centering Prayer are not bad. Rather, they foster a perceived barrier between us and God.

The second lesson is the necessity of opening the door. This is the goal. Is the occupant willing to let go of a situation with which he is familiar and open the door? Having the door closed may have served some worthy purpose in the past, but that is no longer the case. The closed door limits what the person inside can do and can know about the world. Will the person let go? In contemplative prayer, we are faced with the same question. Will we let go of our ordinary and familiar thoughts and be open to God?

The third lesson is about what happens when the door is opened. The visitor enters. And that makes all the difference. The person on the inside begins to experience a loving relationship that banishes aloneness and separation. The occupant now has a friend who comes over for dinner. Something as simple as opening the door has changed his reality.

Centering Prayer offers us the hope of a life-changing experience. When we are open to thoughts and let them go, opening to God becomes a real possibility. Our reality changes as we move from a shallow existence to one of profound depth.

The Virtue of Open-Mindedness

In previous chapters, we have examined familiar sounding character traits like courage, hope, humility, and so on. The topic of this section is new and different. It has only been within the past ten years that Christian philosophers have added *open-mindedness* to their list of virtues.[8] In this section, we will examine what it means to be open-minded and how this quality is associated with Centering Prayer.

Close-Mindedness

Sometimes we can learn a lot about a quality by examining its opposite. Here, we will do that by examining the antithesis of being open-minded—being close-minded.

Understanding how the mind works provides some context for studying the trait of close-mindedness. How does the mind operate? First, the mind likes to reduce complicated features of the world down to simple pairs of opposites—up versus down, in versus out, before versus after, and so on. Second, the mind organizes information into the form of a story—*my* story. This sense of ownership naturally evokes an impression of rightness. Finally, the mind assigns emotions to what we think. These emotions imbue our beliefs with a sense of truth. Our worldview not only appears right but feels right.

This summary overview of how the mind works provides a brief description of what it means to be close-minded: I am right and you are wrong; my story is true and yours is false; and my ideas feel good but yours don't.

Open-Mindedness

People with open minds do not feel compelled to sort ideas into two buckets, such as true versus false. They neither have to be right nor argue that the other person is wrong. The open-minded person offers space for more than one point of view and one story.

Open-minded people are aware of the tricks of the mind. They understand that the mind swiftly grabs onto an idea and holds it tight. They know the mind is quick to develop a case and offer judgment. Therefore, they notice these tendencies and then let them go. They think that just because it seems right to me, it may not be, or that even though it feels right to me, it may not be.

Don't get me wrong; open-minded people are not wishy-washy. Having an open mind does not rule out strong convictions. Robert Roberts and Jay Wood note that "the firm person is, in general, more tenacious with respect to the beliefs that are closer to the center and less so as the outer periphery is reached."[9]

This description presents the image of a circle. There is the center and everything outside the center. At the center, which is relatively small, people hold firmer positions. However, as they move further from the center, they are willing to adjust their beliefs in the light of new knowledge. For example, we let go of old beliefs that the world was flat or that medical doctors didn't need to wash their hands before surgery.

It is possible to be firm in our convictions yet open-minded. People with open minds are willing to listen to those who disagree with them. They are not afraid to understand competing viewpoints. They are able to consider opposing perspectives and revise their ideas accordingly. They can accept having their position criticized. They don't become defensive or angry when their tenets are challenged. They are confident in their own beliefs, while still able to acknowledge that they might be mistaken.

Ultimately, when we are open-minded, we are like the person who "opens the door" (cf. Rev 3:20). We remove the boundary between ourselves and the other person who doesn't view the world the way we do. We remove the barriers of "I'm right and you're wrong," "What I believe is true, but what you believe is false." We refrain from closing our mind. We move from judgment to acceptance, from reaction to receptivity, from control to freedom.

Centered Living

Initially, Centering Prayer may seem to be only about silence. The disciplines of opening and letting go may seem to be rather passive. On the contrary, as Keating observes, "contemplative prayer is a preparation for action."[10] The lessons we have gathered so far in this chapter equip us to interact more lovingly with others, and applying those lessons is Centered Living.

Openness is at the heart of good relationships. In fact, as Paul Wadell notes, "friendships are possible only when we are willing to open our lives to others."[11] There are numerous ways to open our lives to others, but here, in this chapter, we are focused on opening our minds. We want to open our minds and make room for the differing views of others—the opposite of being closed.

In what follows, I am returning to two concepts that are fundamental to Centering Prayer—*opening* and *letting go*—and exploring them within the context of relationships.

Opening

As we have noted earlier, openness is receptivity.[12] When we are receptive, we are open to what the other person thinks and believes. Our neighbor's views don't have to conform to our ideas of what's correct. We refrain from judging a stranger, or even loved one, as wrong. Others don't have to embrace our ideas. Instead, we are open to receiving their values and beliefs.

Daniel Siegel writes that "openness is an embrace of uncertainty."[13] Uncertainty goes against the grain. It goes against the brain. You will recall that the mind likes things to be simple, that is, everything separated into one of two buckets. The mind likes certainty. However, when we are receptive, we are willing to entertain ideas that are different, beliefs that are unfamiliar, concepts that open us up to new possibilities.

Letting Go

Openness and letting go are interconnected. Openness is about letting go. According to Russ Harris, there are three things that we must let go of in relationships: our stories, being right, and control.[14]

The mind likes to tell stories. Some of our narratives about others are useful, but many are unhelpful. Negative stories about others lead to closed doors. Accounts that focus on people's flaws and failings result in separation. For the sake of our relationships, we need to let go of stories that judge and close others out.

The mind likes to be right. An argument that I frequently hear during couples therapy is about who is right. Each partner is wedded to the belief that his or her version of reality is the correct one. Each one is convinced that his or her way of doing things is better. This attitude was once captured by a husband who announced, "We wouldn't have to be here in therapy if my wife just realized that my way is right."

Letting go of our need to be right comes from developing a different attitude toward the mind. The mind is not the arbiter of truth that we often think it is. We wish we could see everything clearly... but we don't. Instead, our mind has only a cloudy view of the truth. Capturing this perspective of the mind, Paul writes, "For now we see in a mirror dimly.... Now I know only in part" (1 Cor 13:12).

We release our grip on being right when we stop confusing our thoughts with the truth. Accepting our limitations when it comes to ascertaining the truth helps us to put our beliefs into perspective. We begin to communicate our thoughts as opinions, perspectives, beliefs, and interpretations. Replacing the language of "I am right" with "My perspective is..." can radically alter the nature of your relationship. We must stop battling with others over who is right. Instead, we must make room for the other person's opinions.

Finally, we need to let go of our need to control. Haven't we learned in Centering Prayer that our first reaction to a thought is to control it?[15] In our attempt to exercise power over a thought, we try to resist it or to hold on to it. However, openness is about first receiving, and then letting go. As Keating observes, "This prayer is an exercise in letting go of everything."[16] In Centering Prayer, we simply put ourselves at God's disposal. The consequences are up to God.

We need to let go of control, not only when we Center, but also within the context of our relationships. Harris contends that "the truth is that we're all control freaks at heart; we all like to get what we want."[17] And, what we want is certainty. However, within relationships, things don't always have to go the way we want or according to our plan.

Conclusion

We conclude this chapter by returning to the image of a closed door portrayed in the Book of Revelation. The occupant of the house was faced with a life-changing question: Will I open the door and let the visitor enter, or will I keep it closed? If I let the guest in, my life won't be so tidy and predictable. Things will no longer be under my control. Everything will lose its certainty.

We are the person in that story. We have the wonderful opportunity in prayer and in relationships to be open. An open mind reveals an entirely new world. Letting go of control unlocks all kinds of novel possibilities. Most important, just as I learned on my first trip to Spain, learning to receive offers us passage into new and loving relationships.

10

PRUDENCE

For several minutes I had been watching a farmer behind his horse as he plowed a field. When he stopped for a short break, I decided that this was my opportunity for striking up a conversation. Since my heritage lies in the rural South and I have a small garden of my own, I wanted to learn more about farming from this expert. Our conversation naturally drifted to the topic of plowing.

There are a few things I took away from our talk. The gray-haired man explained how to make your first furrow. It involves setting a stake some distance away in the field, making sure that the pole is visible. Then, as you walk, always keep your eyes focused on that stake. Attending to something in the distance ensures a straight furrow.

Based on what he said, the person plowing must make good choices. It is important to keep a slow, steady pace as you walk through the field. Keep in mind that the horse is supposed to do most of the hard work. To accomplish this, make certain that the reins on the horse are of the right length and the proper tension. I recall the farmer telling me to be prepared for the natural barriers that might be encountered in the field, such as roots, stones, or even nests of ground hornets.

The wise farmer made it clear that plowing with a horse takes a variety of skills. But this was the phrase that stood out: "Using a plow requires a gentle touch." In other words, you don't have to fight with the plow. In the end, I was left with the idea that the skill of the plowman comes down to one main thing—the time spent behind the plow. Plowing was all about the practice.

Centering Prayer

This story illustrates some of the basic elements of Centering Prayer. It is about watching, keeping your eye on something in the distance, making good choices, and executing the right actions.

Centering Prayer as Watching

Jesus said, "Stay awake and pray" (Matt 26:41). According to Keating, these words capture the essence of Centering Prayer.[1] Prayer is about watching. It is about keeping your eye on a target or destination.

What is the goal of Centering Prayer? This question is vital. Some people make the mistake of assuming that we are attempting to suppress our thoughts or trying to make our mind go blank. That's not the goal at all. We are keeping our eyes on something much more important—a personal relationship with God. Keating reminds us that Centering Prayer is a process that leads, if we are open, to union with God.[2]

In Centering Prayer, as in plowing, our attention is set on something in the distance. In other words, we are oriented in a specific direction, and that is toward God. Nothing will distract us from our long-range goal. Barriers along the way won't sidetrack us. What if my mind were full of anxious thoughts while I Centered today? What if I found my time of prayer slow and boring? The events of today's Centering don't derail us, because our eyes are focused on something in the distance. Keating reminds us that the "long-range goal is the cultivation of friendship"[3] with God.

Centering Prayer is about seeing. We are looking for or watching for God. Indeed, St. Augustine's famous *Confessions* opens with the observation that "our heart is restless until it rests in you," which is similar to "a loving gaze of the human spirit toward God."[4] What we are looking for in contemplative prayer is the face of God. In the Old Testament, the Psalmist proclaims, "Your face, LORD, do I seek" (Psalm 27:8). In the New Testament, the writer of Hebrews encourages us to look to Jesus (cf. Heb 12:2). Even Paul picks up on this theme of seeing God "face to face" (1 Cor 13:12).

It seems as though we were made for face-to-face contact. In Centering Prayer, we are not only watching God, but God is watching us. Our eyes are on God, and God is looking at us. In contemplation, the loving gaze goes both ways.

Centering Prayer as Choosing

In Centering Prayer, we, like the plowman, encounter many barriers as we journey toward our goal. There are many distractions during our daily prayer. Our attention is constantly captured by typical thought patterns. Without our permission, our mind distracts us with some thought that blocks our opening to God.

At some point, we notice the distracting thought and are then faced with a choice. For example, this morning as I Centered, my mind was composing a message to my supervisor at work. I was far along in the process before I even noticed what was happening. My mind had come up with two questions, and my mind had even decided the order in which to present the questions. Prior to noticing this thought process, I was not free to choose. Freedom to choose only came when I became aware of the thoughts occupying my mental space. Now, I was free to make a choice. I could either keep thinking about the message or I could choose to return my mind to my original intention—being open to God.

We revisit turning points like this many times during Centering Prayer—"Will I watch and pray or will I engage in my typical thought process?" In Centering Prayer, we make the choice of turning our eyes toward God by using a sacred word. As Keating reminds us, "By returning to the sacred word, you reaffirm your choice to converse with God and to be united to Him."[5] What are we choosing? We are resolving to return our attention to God's presence.

Centering Prayer as Action

Centering Prayer is about taking appropriate action. We not only make choices that turn us in the right direction—toward God—but we also engage in actions that carry us toward our long-range goal. We not only watch God, but we make use of practices that move us closer to God. In previous chapters, we have identified some of these behaviors: opening, attending, and receiving.

Nevertheless, we must remember our role or place. It is impossible to reach our goal—a relationship with God—on our own. Our own efforts are incapable of bringing us face-to-face with God. Instead of Centering Prayer being a time of hard work and effort, Keating calls it "a very gentle kind of activity."[6]

What is this gentle kind of activity? Our primary task is simply to show up every day for our time of Centering. We say to God, "Here I am. I am here to give you my attention." Everything that follows this is up to God. As Keating notes, "The more God does and the less you do, the better the prayer."[7]

In Centering Prayer we use specific practices, but we should never exert too much effort. Instead, we must primarily focus on one thing—showing up. Keating notes that "the essential discipline is to do it every day."[8] The only "no-no" in Centering Prayer is skipping our daily time of interior silence. Beyond that, we should not put too much pressure on ourselves. We should never mistake watching someone we love as hard work.

The Virtue of Prudence

The farmer I talked to had the primary purpose of plowing the field. But, outside of his awareness, his work was producing other consequences. For example, he was getting good exercise and building muscle. The same thing happens when we pray. Our chief aim is to spend time with God in silence. However, something else is happening. We are building character. One particular trait associated with the contemplative practices of watching, choosing, and acting is the virtue of *prudence*.

According to Aquinas, prudence is defined as knowing that which is good and acting to bring about that good thing. According to Jay Wood, prudence consists of three elements: accurate *perception*, good *judgment*, and appropriate *action*.[9] Let us now explore these fundamental aspects of prudence.

Prudence as Good Perception

Prudence is about learning to see. It is about seeing things rightly, seeing the world as it truly is.[10] However, we are confronted with an inherent human weakness, and that is that human vision lacks clarity. Our eyes are often blinded to the truth. Jesus was well aware of this aspect of the human condition when he asked his disciples, "Do you still not perceive or understand? Are your hearts hardened? Do you have eyes, and fail to see?" (Mark 8:17–18).

How do we respond to the problem of poor perception? From what Jesus is asking, it seems that the issue is related to the heart. We need a change of heart. Paul captures this idea when he writes, "I pray [that] ... with the eyes of your heart enlightened, you may know what is the hope to which he has called you" (Eph 1:18). Paul proffers that clear vision is associated with the orientation of our heart, a heart directed toward God. Notice in this passage that Paul connects seeing with knowledge. Prudence is about learning to see with an enlightened heart.

Ultimately, prudence is about focusing our vision on the right thing. Therefore, prudence is called an "aiming" virtue.[11] Prudence is about picking a good destination and maintaining our focus on that objective. We keep our eyes focused on the end. That is what we do when we Center. We set our eyes upon the goal of relating with God.

Prudence as Good Judgment

Prudence is also about good judgment. We are being prudent when we make choices that are in the best interests of ourselves and others. When I am hiking, my mind offers me two perceptions of the poisonous snake—it either looks like a snake, or it appears to be a stick. I can choose to avoid it or to pick it up. It is obvious that making the best choice is dependent upon seeing the situation clearly.

Making good choices is connected to both prudence and freedom. We are not free to make just any choice. Freedom is "the power to choose the good."[12] When we make good choices, we are not only free, we are being prudent. In fact, we are truly free and prudent when we are choosing to love God, our neighbor, and our self.

My mind is always offering me opposing viewpoints or thoughts about situations. Which thought will I choose? In Centering Prayer, my mind presents me with an ordinary thought or with the thought of being present to God. Which will I choose? Obviously, one choice is better than the other. Dallas Willard writes, "The power to choose our thoughts is . . . our most basic freedom, our first and primary freedom."[13]

Prudence as Good Action

Finally, prudence is about appropriate action—acting in such a way as to bring about our own and others' well-being.[14] It is not enough simply to know the right course of action. The prudent person acts in such a way as to bring about good ends. Prudence sees the good end, chooses the best means of achieving that end, and then skillfully executes the action that brings about that end. Clear vision and good choices by themselves are not sufficient. Prudence also has to do with *action*.

The nature of prudence is illustrated in two parables of Jesus. One parable is that of the wise builder (cf. Matt 7:24–27), while the second is about five wise virgins (cf. Matt 25:1–13). The wise builder combined good vision, good choices, and good action when he constructed his house on a foundation of solid rock. The wise virgins connected good thinking, good decision-making, and good behavior when they went out into the evening not only with lamps but also with jars full of oil.

The story of Jesus's visit with Mary and Martha also presents a picture of prudence (cf. Luke 10:38–42). The two women had two different views of the event, they made divergent choices and, as a result, they took opposing actions. Martha was concentrating on the task of entertaining her guests, while Mary's goal was to engage in conversation with Jesus, carefully listening. Observing the situation, Jesus commented, "Mary has *chosen* the better part" (v. 42). Mary was clearly demonstrating prudence on this occasion.

What actions will we take with regard to Centering Prayer? We can either show up for our daily time of interior silence or we can go off and do something else for those twenty minutes. We have the option of attending to God or doing something else. These are simple behaviors but they can make a huge difference. Good actions, along with good perception and good choices, can produce a crop of prudence in our lives.

Centered Living

The things we learn from Centering Prayer and prudence have direct implications for our relationships. By applying what we learn to our daily lives we becoming proficient in Centered Living. Centered Living entails how we perceive others, making good choices that benefit our friends, and employing good actions that have a positive impact on those around us. In this section, we will examine how these learned lessons contribute to the welfare of our relationships.

The Importance of Being Seen

At the center of our most important human relationships is face-to-face encounters. Within the first hours of our life, we start searching out the faces around us, and for some reason we prefer our parents' faces. Louis Cozolino writes, "Vision, in general, and the emotionally expressive face, in particular, have come to play central roles in human bonding.... The sounds, feel, and sight of the mother's expressive face elevate dopamine and endorphin levels, making the mother the infant's primary source of enjoyment and satisfaction."[15] Throughout our life, we seek genuine face-to-face encounters.

The look on your face communicates a wealth of information.[16] For example, your smile sends the message that you are making space for a stranger; you are inviting a loved one to approach. However, when you avoid eye contact or send a look of disapproval, others know to keep their distance.

Prolonged eye contact—or gazing—is a clear signal of love. C. S. Lewis expresses this when he writes that "lovers are normally face to face, absorbed in each other."[17] Why is it that love shows itself in this way, that is, when we maintain eye contact with someone? Because, when we gaze at others, they feel safe and whole. Words are not necessary. Our loving eyes are saying all that they want to hear—that they are accepted, cherished, and loved.

The Power of Choosing

Successful relationships are the result of cultivating thoughtful choices.[18] Our mind is constantly generating thoughts within the context of our relationships. Some of our ideas about others are unhelpful, while some are helpful. The important process of making a choice begins with the awareness of thoughts. Once we notice our thoughts, then we are able to make a choice.

Let me suggest a couple of practical ways for choosing thoughts that will promote better relationships with others. One tactic is to catch and challenge negative thinking. For example, if you are thinking that someone is mean, then call into question that belief. Dispute the thought by raising the possibility that maybe the person isn't mean. Second, choose to remind yourself that the thought is simply a *thought*. Instead of assuming that your thought that "she is selfish," is undoubtedly true, consider perhaps that it is a mistaken notion.

The Skill of Perspective Taking

Earlier in this chapter we noted that interpretations of events are frequently faulty. The remedy for this problem is the skill of *perspective taking*. Perspective taking is defined as the ability to imagine what the other person is going through.[19] In other words, it is the ability to see a situation from a viewpoint that is not one's own. As we engage this process, we must attempt to distance ourselves from our own perception long enough to explore and understand the other person's viewpoint.

For example, after arriving home from work, I enter the room where my wife is seated and notice that she remains focused on her art project instead of welcoming me home with a hug. My mind presents two thoughts: (1) she is at a crucial point in her work and can't be distracted; or (2) she is not interested in me. In this scenario, if I choose to go with the second thought, then I have committed an error in perception.

How do I check out my perception?[20] First, I can internally describe her behavior without evaluating it: "She isn't making eye contact with me." Next, I need to identify the two disparate thoughts that she either doesn't care about me or that she is afraid of getting distracted. Finally, it is important to ask my wife for clarification: "Are you too busy to stop right now? Are you happy to see me?"

Ultimately, perspective taking is a skill that brings us to where we started this section. Our loved ones and friends want to be seen and seen accurately. Co-workers and neighbors want us to see them in a good light. The way we see others and the manner in which we choose to think about them makes all the difference in the world.

III

BEHAVIORAL VIRTUES

11

DILIGENCE

I was on a trip with my family out west. After visiting several national parks, we arrived at the Grand Canyon. I was on the rim as the sun went down. I was not prepared for the beauty of that sunset. The brilliant red and orange glow extended across the horizon. The contrasts of light and shadow were incredible. The sunset was both tranquil and gorgeous.

The wonder of those minutes was beyond my control. It would be ridiculous to think that I could do anything to add to the glory of that sunset. My role was minimal, but I had a part to play. It was important that I be present there and pay attention. My chief task was to be open to the celestial show. It was up to nature to do the rest.

At that moment, if anyone had called me to my favorite meal, I would have completely ignored them. I was captured by the beauty of those fleeting minutes. All I wanted to do was to freeze the sunset and remain in that moment forever. But that was not to be. Gradually, the sun set and darkness overtook the night sky. However, that moment remains for me, because I am still affected by it today.

Centering Prayer

Contemplative prayer is a journey into the wild unknown. There are so many possibilities. Centering Prayer is a process of radical change. Our consciousness opens to a totally new level of being. We traverse the gap between the false self and the true self. We exchange an old heart for a new one. And, most of all, we become open to the love of God. All of these changes are captured in the word *transformation*. Thomas Keating writes, "The purpose of contemplative prayer is to facilitate the process of inner transformation."[1]

Three Responses to Centering Prayer

There are two common approaches to contemplative prayer. The first is to attempt to control it. In other words, we try to manufacture this experience and hold on to it. Some people are looking for a simple set of exercises for turning on or possessing the presence of God. However, no such process exists. As Gerald May writes, "As with love, the more we try to control prayer, the less prayer can happen."[2]

Centering Prayer is not a self-improvement method. It is not some strategy for independently achieving our desired end.[3] For example, it is not like learning to fish and then expecting to get predictable results. It is not a technique that we apply on our own. Centering Prayer is not a solo venture.

The second familiar approach to contemplative prayer is to quickly walk away in defeat. Why would we abandon a process so full of possibility? I think the answer is that we find it so hard. Let's not kid ourselves. Centering Prayer invites suffering. It is difficult to sit with thoughts that are being endlessly supplied by the unconscious. We let go of one thought, only to quickly experience the emergence of another one. Our moments of silence are relentlessly pierced by the arrow of a new thought. We wish we could control our thoughts, but we can't. So, what do we do? We give up.

Perhaps we wouldn't be so quick to walk away if we realized that, in some mysterious way, God is using our suffering in the change process. If only we could grasp the significance of learning to detach from thoughts. When we catch a thought and return to our sacred word, our mind and heart are being altered. When we notice a shiny idea and let it go, something miraculous happens. Both thoughts and silence are part of the transformation process.

But, there is another choice. The third approach begins with the realization that transformation is God's work. This leads to an acceptance of our need to cooperate with the process of transformation. For example, suppose I need a haircut. I know that my hairdresser is the only one capable of doing the job. She is trained and qualified to accomplish what I desperately need but cannot do on my own. There are, however, ways in which I can assist. I can show up on time and comply with her requests as she cuts my hair. Compared to what she does, my part is effortless.

Gentle Activity

Keating describes Centering Prayer as "an exercise in effortlessness."[4] What does he mean? Here, he is equating the term *effort* with the concept of *trying*, as in "I am trying to make something happen." Remember that "transformation is completely God's work. We can't do anything to make it happen."[5] In this context, the term "effortlessness" means that we are adopting an attitude of dependency on God. We assume that God is doing the heavy lifting; our job is simply to cooperate in a small way.

So, does this mean that we to do nothing? Keating reminds us that "practicing this prayer is not doing nothing. It is a very gentle kind of activity."[6] Our task does not require very much effort but it does require some. We are supposed to engage in suitable exercises, which Keating calls "appropriate efforts."[7]

Some of the key "gentle activities" of Centering Prayer include: consenting to God's presence; listening to God's silence; returning to the sacred word; letting go of thoughts; waiting on God; and resting in God's arms. In fact, Keating adds that "to receive God is the chief work in contemplative prayer"[8]— just as with my hairdresser, my most important role is showing up. My contribution is small, compared with God's, but it is important nevertheless.

Our part can be compared to the work of opening a door. Keating notes that "it is not a big effort to open the door."[9] Opening a door is a simple and uncomplicated process, but this step is essential. With the door closed, nothing can be accomplished. However, when I open the door, I am making way for the work of my divine guest.

Joint Activity

It is misleading to think of contemplative prayer as something done either by God or by ourselves. The practice of silence is not an *either/or* proposition;[10] rather, it is a joint activity. We are responsible for our actions; God is responsible for God's. Mysteriously, by the grace of God's Spirit, our actions— waiting, opening, listening, and so on—are actually abilities or gifts given to us by God. Centering Prayer is a *both/and* proposition. We exercise certain behaviors while recognizing that those actions are really gifts of God.

Appropriate effort entails doing our part, even if it is ever so humble. God is doing most of the work, but we have essential tasks, and as we engage in appropriate efforts we recognize that the gift of contemplation is a joint activity.

In the next section, we will examine how the basic principles of Centering Prayer enhance the important character trait called diligence.

The Virtue of Diligence

The Merriam Webster dictionary defines diligence as "steady, earnest, and energetic effort; devoted and painstaking work and application to accomplish an undertaking." The word stems from the Latin word *diligere* meaning "to respect, esteem, love." Diligence is about being responsible in carrying out the tasks associated with the highest goal of all—love.

The Vice Associated with Diligence

To better understand the nature of diligence, we will first turn to its opposite. According to Aquinas, the vice associated with diligence is *sloth*. In modern times, sloth has most frequently been linked to the notion of being lazy, but this definition is misleading. The traditional definition of sloth—apathy or indifference—reveals a deeper meaning. One connotation of the term is being lazy about love. *Sloth* is actually the lack of love.

Sloth is a failure to receive love. But why would one refuse love? Rebecca DeYoung provides us with some insight.[11] Slothful people want to stay the way they are. They object to transformation because it demands a new view of self. For the slothful person, change seems too hard, too demanding. The price of love seems too steep. Renouncing the old self seems too painful. The practices that draw one closer to God appear too difficult.[12]

What does the slothful person do when the way of love seems too threatening? Such a person steers clear of that pathway. This avoidance can take one of two distinct forms. Aquinas identifies them as restlessness and laziness.[13] These two signs of resistance to love are polar opposites: on the one end, the slothful person can stay busy, living a hectic life, while on the other end, sloth can drag the person into inactivity.

We typically associate sloth with the second form, that is, physical inactivity. But this view is inaccurate. Sloth speaks to something deeper than one's external behavior, that is, whether one is lazy in work or not. Instead, it addresses an inner condition. In his resistance to the demands of love, the slothful person pulls back in aversion from the only thing that can fulfill him—love.

A Story of Diligence

Jesus's parable of the talents illustrates the difference between sloth and diligence (cf. Matt 25:14–30). In this story, a man entrusts his property to three servants. One is entrusted with five talents,[14] another with three talents, and the third with one talent. According to the story, the first and second servants are described by the master as "trustworthy in a few things" (vv. 21 and 23). However, the third servant is characterized as "lazy" (v. 26).

At first glance, this story appears to be about work, but when we dig deeper, we discover that it is a parable about love. The narrative depicts a master desirous of a deep bond with his servants. This becomes obvious when he utters the words, "Enter into the joy of your master" (vv. 21 and 23). The master is primarily interested in establishing a loving relationship with his servants.

The master and the first two servants form an intimate connection, but this is not the case with the final servant. Out of fear, the last servant freezes. He puts forth no effort to respond to the master's love. The master, despite his desire for closeness, is unable to overcome the third servant's resistance to love.

Diligence is not only about a shared relationship; it is about a shared activity. The two diligent servants, through their investments, are being responsible with the talents entrusted to them. They exercise appropriate effort so that the money grows. But where had the money come from in the first place? Who had provided the two men with training in financial matters? The resources and education originated with the master. The master fulfilled his role—a greater one—while the two servants were "trustworthy in a few things."

The virtue of diligence recognizes that friendship with God is not a one-way street. Instead, a relationship of love requires joint activity. Paul admonishes the church in Philippi: "Work out your own salvation with fear and trembling; for it is God who is at work in you, enabling you both to will and to work for his good pleasure" (Phil 2:12–13). Peter, making a similar observation, writes, "His divine power has given us everything needed for life and godliness.... For this very reason, you must *make every effort* to support your faith with goodness" (2 Peter 1:3–7). We are reminded in these passages that we are not called to toil alone. Instead, we are always working with God.

The Hard Work of Love

While sloth avoids love, the virtue of diligence moves us toward the hard work of love. Diligence is a disciplined effort to learn the way of love. With this virtue, we stay and face God's invitation to be transformed. We accept the real work that goes along with a commitment to love, and we willingly engage in the daily practices that are designed to strengthen our friendship with God.

Centered Living

Let us now examine how Centering Prayer impacts our daily life regarding this virtue of diligence. I am particularly interested in practical ways of connecting the lessons of Centering Prayer to our relationships.

As we noted earlier, Centering Prayer is a process of taking a good, hard look at oneself. Am I open to transformation? Am I willing to change? It is also an invitation to consider my part. What do I need to do to accomplish the desired outcome? Finally, Centering Prayer is a door to mutuality and reciprocity. Am I trying to accomplish this on my own? How well am I working with the Divine Other?

Applying these principles to human relationships involves *responsibility*. Psychologists tell us that being responsible is an indispensable ingredient in relational success.[15] When we are being responsible, we are acknowledging our part. Our task is to control our own feelings and behaviors. Furthermore, responsibility engenders an attitude of being-in-this-together. When we are being responsible, we acknowledge the impact we have on others. And when we become aware that we are falling short, we become focused on our need to change.

Rights versus Responsibilities

Being responsible is the opposite of being focused on our rights. (Here, I am not talking about basic human rights such as the right to life, freedom of expression, education, etc.) An orientation toward rights leads us to concentrate on what others can do for us. How can you please me? What do you need to do to meet my expectations? How can you make me feel loved, important, and the center of your attention? A rights mentality naturally leads us to monitor and judge other's behavior toward us.

An emphasis on our rights moves us in the direction of "individualism."[16] This is not an "us" mentality. Instead, the focus is centered on me. As long as you are meeting my needs, I will remain in this relationship. However, as soon as you start disappointing me, I might walk away. I might choose to do something more rewarding and less challenging.

The final servant in Jesus's parable of the talents demonstrated these signs of individualism. He saw himself as independent from the master. He could bury the money, walk away, and give no further thought to the master. He was on his own. He assumed that he could retreat to his private place and shut the door.

Responsibility is the opposite of individualism. When we are being responsible, we acknowledge that our lives are not separate and private. In fact, we are not truly capable of retreat. Our lives are intertwined with the lives of others.[17] Because our lives overlap, we are not only being impacted by others, but we are impacting them as well. As a result of this awareness, we do what we can to contribute to the welfare of others.

Reactivity versus Responsibility

Being responsible is the opposite of being reactive. When we are being reactive, our comeback to others is automatic. Our behavior is impulsively directed by our emotions. The behaviors that are typical of reactive people are fight or flight, attack or withdraw.

Responsible people, however, opt to restrain their automatic impulses. They push the pause button before reacting to the other person. Then, they think through the situation, choosing behaviors that are driven neither by anger nor by fear. People who are being responsible continue to wait, choose wise actions, and keep their ears open.

Mona Fishbane offers us four practical elements of responsibility: awareness, thoughtfulness, flexibility, and choice.[18] With *awareness*, we observe the thoughts and feelings that automatically enter our minds. Awareness is about learning to notice and let go of these impulsive reactions. When we are *thoughtful*, we are willing to consider our companion's viewpoint. When we are *flexible*, we insert a space between our initial impulse and our action. During this pause, we take time to consider various behavioral options. This process leads us to *choosing*, making a responsible choice.

Conclusion

We conclude this chapter with a brief portrait of a responsible person. First, responsible people are dedicated to the hard work of love. They adopt an attitude of self-awareness, that is, awareness of their own thoughts, emotions, and behavior, and they readily adapt them when necessary. Instead of running away or fighting when a relationship stalls, they voluntarily embrace a posture of responsibility by assessing their own role in the problem. And finally, unwilling to see themselves as independent from others, they rejoice at the possibilities of relationships based upon joint activity and mutual responsibility.

12

PATIENCE

My heart leapt when I saw her step out of the plane. There she was in her summery, white outfit and blue sandals. Her hair was cut in a cute, short style. I could hardly contain myself as I paced back and forth, eagerly expecting her to come through the door to the waiting area any minute. This was the moment I had been waiting for. It had been a year since Ana had set off to finish her final year of studies at the University of Madrid. Now she was returning. For a year, we had corresponded regularly by letters. Now, we were going to be together again.

I recently asked Ana, "What was it like to know that I was waiting for you during that time?" She gave a thoughtful response. She said that the waiting acted like an invisible line or rope between the two of us. It provided us with a connection. It drew us toward one another. It shaped our goal for the future—being reunited. It gave us hope that we would actually be together at some point.

Centering Prayer

As we have already noted, the message we communicate during Centering Prayer is, "Here I am, waiting."[1] There is something ordinary and mundane about waiting, isn't there? We want the desired moment to come sooner, but it doesn't. We want to change the timeline, but we can't. We can only wait. But the person we are waiting for is exciting and captivating. That is why we continue to wait.

A Story of Waiting

In the parable of the watchful slaves, Jesus speaks of the importance of waiting: "Be dressed for action and have your lamps lit; be like those who are *waiting* for their master to return from the wedding banquet, so that they may open the door for him as soon as he comes and knocks" (Luke 12:35–36).

The first thing we notice in this parable is that the servants are waiting for someone. The same is true in Centering Prayer—we are waiting for God. According to Thomas Keating, Centering Prayer is about "waiting for God without going away, giving the usual time to prayer, and putting up with what goes on in the imagination."[2] He adds that these simple practices "will lead to a complete change of heart."[3] That's what waiting does; it transforms our hearts.

The second thing we notice in this account is that the servants undoubtedly experience distractions while they wait. I imagine that they have been on standby for many hours. Of course, other things must have come up, but the servants remain alert for the sound of the master's knock on the door.

We also encounter disturbances when we wait on God during Centering Prayer. A continuous line of thoughts clamor for our attention while we wait on God. Will we get so tired of all the disorder that we quit waiting, that we get up and go away? Or, will we keep waiting without going away, putting up with the contents of our mind?

The third thing we become aware of is that waiting for a person is dramatically different from waiting for God. The servants who were waiting for their master immediately knew when he arrived. But it is not this way with God. God's appearance is not marked with flashing lights, blowing horns, or even banging on the door. When God arrives, it doesn't even register in our conscious minds.

Waiting is a mysterious process. You are waiting for God, but don't even recognize union with God when it occurs. Keating observes that "you can't possibly know by means of any human faculty; so it is useless to expect anything. You don't know and can't know what you are waiting for."[4] You only know in retrospect—once a conscious thought appears—that you have been in a fleeting period of silence. Now, you begin all over again, that is, waiting for God.

Characteristics of Waiting

Waiting is an active process. Keating writes that "the waiting process is a preparation for moments of divine union."[5] For example, what if you are planning to go out on a date? You won't be just sitting there waiting for your date to arrive. No, you'll be getting yourself ready, putting on your clothes and getting prepared.

When we have a date with God—Centering Prayer—we are preparing for God's presence. As we wait for a moment of silence, we are addressing the thought that entered our mind. We are not resisting it, holding onto it, or reacting to it. Instead, we are accepting it and letting it go. We are waiting for the thought to pass. And perhaps, when it does, we enter into another moment of silence. However, instead of silence, maybe another thought arises. Then, we prepare for God's presence by accepting and letting go of that thought. That is the nature of Centering Prayer.

Waiting is about time. As we Center, we become attuned to the passage of time. We are lingering with God for a certain number of minutes without going away. We are devoid of expectations. We don't even know what to expect. We are drifting in and out of silence. We let go of the most recent thought and start waiting all over again for God. Perhaps a large stretch of time is spent letting go of thoughts. Just one minute—or even a second—to catch the aroma of God's presence is worth the wait.

Waiting is not easy. Sometimes it is hard to sit with distracting thoughts for a long period. Some thoughts are difficult to accept, so we may resist them. The emotions that accompany memories may be painful and may evoke a reaction. Putting up with the imaginings of our mind for twenty minutes can be trying. We may think that this is not what we wanted— sweet silence—and since we are not getting what we want, we are going to stop. Waiting is about enduring the discomfort and not going away.

The thing that keeps us from leaving is our intention. Our intention reminds us of why we are waiting. We are not waiting for some flashy experience when we Center. No, we are simply being open to God. We are listening for God's knock. We continue to deal with and let go of distractions as they occur. After letting go of a thought, we start waiting all over again for God's gentle tap at the door. That is why we are waiting. We are waiting to open the door.

Gerald May reminds us that "intention is the most significant, the most essential, the most completely human thing about us."[6] Intention is important because it points us and moves us in a certain direction. Intention keeps our actions from being aimless and chaotic. But, with intention, we seek and find the thing that means the most to us.

The Virtue of Patience

Thomas Keating portrays the Centering practice of waiting as training in character. He writes, "It takes great patience to accept the thought and not to be sad because one is prevented from entering that silence. Just start over."[7] For Keating, starting over is the essence of patience.

The virtue of patience has largely been ignored. Stanley Hauerwas observes that patience was not that important to the Greeks or Romans.[8] In fact, it seems that the term was not even in their vocabulary. However, the concept of patience has been important to Christians. The term was prominent in the language of both Jesus and New Testament authors.

A Description of Patience

I define patience as the ability to endure a hardship for the sake of a worthy goal. Notice that this definition has three components: endurance, hardship, and goal. Let's now consider each of these crucial elements.

A key to patience is the concept of *endurance*. Endurance has to do with time. Patience is the virtue that enables us to weather the test of time. This is the reason that patience is often equated with the idea of waiting. Patience helps us hang in there while we are waiting for something to pass or to happen. Because of perseverance, we don't give up.

The second element of patience is *hardship*. Hardship prompts the question: Why do we need patience? Perseverance is necessary because our lives contain suffering. We all deal with obstacles and difficulties in our life. How will we grapple with the pain of life? Will we run away or give up? The virtue of patience enables us to hold on through the hardship.

Patience takes seriously the human experience of suffering and pain. We do not belittle the affliction. We do not deny it. Rather, we admit the anguish. We are not indifferent to it. Suffering is real. However, patience helps us wait for the hurt to pass. Paul, recognizing the connection between pain and patience, wrote, "We also boast in our sufferings, knowing that suffering produces endurance" (Rom 5:3).

Waiting, by itself, does not reveal whether or not a person is patient. For example, suppose John is waiting in line for a free ticket to a concert. We see that John is lined up with his best friends. As he stands by, John is laughing, talking, and having a good time. Waiting in line with his friends is fun. Even if John lingers for two hours for the free ticket, we cannot say that John is patient. Why not? Because he has not been suffering any hardship.

Now, to determine if someone is truly patient, we must consider the third element—that is, the person's *goal*. Is the person waiting in the midst of pain for a worthy goal? Patience requires that a person endure a hardship for something of great value. When we revisit our story of John, the goal is minor—a free ticket. Even if John waited two hours with his friends to achieve his goal, we wouldn't say that he is patient. In fact, he has only really met one of the three conditions for patience.

Let's consider another story about John, one that illustrates the true nature of patience. In this account, John has to wait in line for two hours. When he reaches the endpoint, he will receive paperwork that will allow him to leave the violent and oppressive country in which he is living. John can see that his particular line is one of many that are converging toward the end. He can tell that the lines get crowded and congested as people reach the endpoint, with much pushing and shoving. John is having a hard time, because he is afraid of desperate crowds.

In this story, we see all the elements of patience. John has to endure hardship in order to achieve a worthy goal. He doesn't give up. Rather, he stays put. Despite the obstacles, John is focused on the task at hand. John is voluntarily choosing to put up with the difficulties, to wait in the pain. In this case, we can determine that John is exhibiting patience.

Patience with God

We are quick to admit that patience is required in human relationships, but it is also essential with God. Why do we need patience with God? What does such patience look like?

There are times when God seems absent. Life is presenting us with serious hardships but God seems remote. We have unanswered questions and our beliefs are shaken, but God is silent. The hiddenness of God calls for patience.[9]

What do we do during these periods of time when God feels distant or hidden? Do we reproach God for not living up to our expectations at that moment? Do we fall into despair? Through our impatience, do we react by turning away from God, or even walking away?

This is when we need patience. Patiently, we admit our suffering. Yes, the experience of God's hiddenness is painful. But, with patience, we endure the discomfort for a worthy goal— God's presence. We remember that our goal is a worthy one. We remind ourselves that neither our minds or our emotions

127

are truly capable of perceiving God's presence. By faith—a friend of patience—we remind ourselves that God is present despite the perceived absence.

For me, no other gospel story captures our need for patience with God better than the story of the death of Lazarus (cf. John 11:1–16). While Lazarus was still sick, his sisters—Mary and Martha—sent word to Jesus that Lazarus was ill. After receiving the message, instead of rushing off to be of help, Jesus stayed in Jerusalem. He was only two miles away from the home of the three siblings, but he delayed his trip to Bethany.

By the time Jesus arrived, Lazarus had already been dead for four days, and Martha reacted with anger. Who could blame her? Mary's reaction was different—more like despair. She had just given up on him. "Perhaps he doesn't really care about me," she may have thought.

This is a story that captures our need for patience with God. Mary and Martha are eager for Jesus to show up, to be of assistance. Instead, to their surprise and dismay, Jesus does not respond immediately. Can we relate to them? At times, we also find ourselves in need of God's presence, but he seems hidden. It feels like God stays away. Only patience can get us through these difficult and painful times. We must keep on waiting for God to show up. We can't give up. We can't walk away.

Jesus himself experienced the sense of God's remoteness. During his crucifixion, Jesus cried out, "My God, my God, why have you forsaken me?" (Matt 27:46). What helped Jesus get through this unbearable hardship? In his agony and pain, Jesus must have relied upon the virtue of patience.

Centered Living

Centering Prayer teaches us to be patient with God, but it also equips us for daily living. Unbeknownst to us, while we Center, we are learning to be long-suffering with the people in our lives. Centering Prayer is preparing us for action, and the resulting behavior is called Centered Living.

For a scientific view of patience, we turn here to the discipline of psychology. The concept of patience was ignored by psychology until recently. Pioneers in the psychological study of patience (also called perseverance), Christopher Peterson and Martin Seligman, define patience as finishing what one has started, keeping on going despite obstacles, and sticking to the task.[10] People display patience when they voluntarily continue with a goal-oriented action despite difficulties or discouragement.

Following in the footsteps of Peterson and Seligman, positive psychologist Angela Duckworth has written a very popular book called *Grit*.[11] In this work, Duckworth affirms certain things we know about patience. Patience is about not abandoning a task in the face of difficulties. With patience, we keep on going. And, even when we get knocked down, we get back up and continue with the job at hand. Patience sustains us on the path to our goals.

We must set and patiently pursue goals in our relationships. Have you lost—or never set—your intentions for your marriage, family, friends, and neighbors? Perhaps you started the relationship with a clear direction. You wanted your child or spouse to feel special. You wanted to be a good friend. You wanted to be a loving and caring neighbor. But you have since lost your way.

Goals bring us back to our original target and remind us of the direction in which we want to go. When was the last time that you stopped and asked yourself: What are my goals for my marriage, this friendship, this new acquaintance, and so on?

Without goals, we wind up simply reacting to the latest event. Our behavior is guided by nothing more than how we feel at that moment. When the other person is frustrating or difficult, we say or do the first thing that enters our mind. But this reactive mentality has no long-term direction. It is focused only on the present moment.

We need something more reliable for our relationships. We need clear objectives. We need to regularly return to our goals and intentions. Through our goals and intentions, we continually remind ourselves of our desired endpoint. Of course, at times, we will get lost and head in the wrong direction. But, with patience, we can get reoriented, keep working at it, and endure.

13

TRUTHFULNESS

In chapter 6, we began with a poem by Dietrich Bonhoeffer. Please indulge me as we review four lines from that poem once again:

> Who am I? This one or the other?
> Am I this one today, and tomorrow another?
> Am I both at once?
> Who am I?

What do you see when you look at this poem? Do you see the words, or do you see the white space? Most of us are captured by the text, because our language skills are focused in the left hemisphere—or conscious part—of our brain that prefers words. However, the right hemisphere—or unconscious part—communicates by other means, such as emotion, images, body language, and silence.

In this chapter, we will explore how both words and silence are the stuff of which Centering Prayer is made. In contemplative prayer, we do not dishonor or mistreat words. They don't scare us and we don't fight them. We open ourselves to both words and to the space between words. In contemplative prayer, we learn to reverse our preferences so that silence becomes the desired manner of communicating.

Centering Prayer

Centering Prayer is a conversation with God.[1] Whereas human-to-human communication is often conducted with words, this is not the case when we converse with God. The language of God is the language of silence. As we drop down into interior silence, we enter a dimension beyond words. This is a level where God speaks to our spirit. At this plane, our mind is incapable of hearing the conversation with God.

To be clear, the goal of contemplative prayer is not the absence of words. Instead, Centering Prayer can be characterized as detachment from words. As Thomas Keating notes, "During the entire course of a period of centering prayer, we are slipping in and out of interior silence."[2] At times, our mind is captured by a thought—a grouping of words. But, once that string of words passes, we may enter into a brief period of silence.

At the heart of Centering Prayer is an exercise for letting go of words and moving into silence. The method is described as returning to the sacred word. In a manner that may seem contradictory, we employ a word in our attempt to lay aside words. Keating notes that "the sacred word is a way of letting go of thoughts."[3] In Centering Prayer, we use a word to let go of words. What a paradox!

The Dynamics of the Sacred Word

The mind has two typical responses to thoughts. The first is to grasp them tightly. The second is to resist and push them away. The first reaction reveals an attraction to the idea, while the second one shows contempt for a particular thought.

Use of the sacred word offers us a different way to interact with thoughts. Keating suggests that we "resist no thought, hang on to no thought, react emotionally to no thought...return to the sacred word."[4] Notice the word "return." It is a mild and tranquil word.

How we employ the sacred word is important. It is not some form of weapon used for defeating a thought. We do not use it aggressively or urgently. The passing thought is not bad; it is not our enemy. It is simply distracting us from our original intention. Therefore, with little effort, in a still and peaceful manner, we recall the sacred word. By gently turning our attention to our sacred word, we are able to let go of the distracting thought.

What makes your word sacred? It is sacred because of its intention. The word itself has no special meaning. However, it is sacred because it is pointing you toward an activity that is spiritual. The sacred word can also be described as a *symbol*. A symbol is something that represents something else, as, for example, use of the letter H to stand for the chemical element hydrogen.

What does the sacred word symbolize? In what direction is it pointing us? What is its purpose? Keating maintains that "the sacred word is the symbol of consenting to God's presence."[5] He also notes that "it expresses your intention to open yourself to God."[6] When we become interested in a passing thought, the sacred word serves as a reminder that we are sitting in prayer in order to open ourselves to God. We are communicating with God. We are listening to God's silence, and "by returning to the sacred word," Keating observes, we "reaffirm [our] choice to converse with God."[7]

Listening to God

In Centering Prayer, the sacred word is a specific component of our conversation with God. By helping to move us into

133

silence, the sacred word facilitates two complementary parts of communication—*speaking* and *listening*. In contemplative prayer, we relinquish our role of talking so that God can speak to us in silence. So, letting go of our thoughts gives God the opportunity to talk to us.

Richard Rohr notes that "in the spiritual life it's much more important to know how to listen than to know how to talk."[8] Returning to the sacred word is directly linked to our ability to listen to God. As Keating maintains, "In this prayer, you are listening to God, listening to His silence. Your only activity is the attention that you offer to God either implicitly by letting go of all thoughts or explicitly by returning to the sacred word."[9]

Contemplative prayer is a special type of listening.[10] We are listening to a voice that cannot be heard. We are listening to a discussion that is taking place at the heart of the Trinity. In some unfathomable manner, a dialogue between the Father, Son, and Spirit is passing through us (cf. Rom 8:26; Gal 4:6). And, in some small way, we are joining in this conversation by returning to the sacred word.

The Virtue of Truthfulness

In the first section of this chapter, we have discussed fundamental aspects of communication in Centering Prayer. *Choosing* the right word is necessary. Furthermore, *employing* the right word in the right way is essential. And finally, using the right word for the right *purpose* is all-important. These lessons from Centering Prayer are combined when we consider the virtue of truthfulness.

Stanley Hauerwas asserts that "God has given us a wonderful exercise for training in truthfulness. That exercise is called prayer."[11] This assertion by Hauerwas supports one of the major themes of this book—that we develop virtues within the context of contemplative prayer. Contemplative prayer is not the only site for strengthening character traits—just like a gym is not the only place for building muscles—but it is nevertheless a good one.

Throughout history, philosophical and Christian literature have seldom identified truthfulness as a virtue. This is surprising, given the importance of truthfulness in the Bible. Hauerwas, a contemporary American theologian, argues that truthfulness is the virtue that enables us to communicate well.[12]

What is truthfulness? I define truthfulness as the habit of choosing the *right words*, speaking them in the *right way*, and using them for the *right purpose*. Let us now carefully consider these three aspects of truthfulness.

The Right Words

Truthfulness within the context of verbal communication requires choosing the right words. However, be assured that I am not equating the phrase "right words" with objective reality. We begin with the assumption (supported by science) that the human mind is not capable of ascertaining the whole truth. The truth is that we cannot know the truth. In fact, as Richard Rohr notes, "we are all partial knowers."[13]

I believe in objective reality, but I have doubts about our ability to know it. Of course, we want to know the truth, and we desire the ability to put everything into two categories— this is black and that is white; this is true and that is false. However, the mind has numerous weaknesses and biases that interfere with this goal.

The discipline of psychology identifies multiple sources

of bias and distortion that lead us down the road to poor judgments and inaccurate conclusions.[14] One of these sources has to do with the fact that much of the work of the mind is done outside of awareness. Without our knowing it, our unconscious mind is forming its own conclusions and preferences. We think we are carefully weighing all the evidence, while in reality we are simply coming up with reasons to support what our unconscious mind has already concluded on its own.

There is a second flaw in our thinking that interferes with our desire to know the truth. Since the mind likes to simplify its tasks, it takes shortcuts. One of these shortcuts involves distorting incoming information so that it fits with our pre-existing biases, expectancies, and preferences. If I already believe something, my mind only allows in information that supports that preconceived idea. This requires less mental effort than having to reconsider and reevaluate what I already consider to be true. Essentially, these mental shortcuts increase the risk of errors and mistakes in thinking.

The "right words," then, are not actually reflections of objective reality. We express our acknowledgment of this fact by including in our statements phrases such as:

In my opinion...
From my perspective...
I believe...but I might be mistaken.
It is okay if we believe two different things.
I have concluded...but I might be wrong.
The way I remember it is...

Ultimately, we are better at choosing the right words when we let go of our need to be right. From this place of humility, we make greater strides toward truthfulness.

The Right Way

Words matter. Because our lives are intermingled, our words have a significant impact on the listener. As St. James says, "How great a forest is set ablaze by a small fire! And the tongue is a fire...a restless evil, full of deadly poison" (Jas 3:5–7). A word is a powerful spark of fire. Recognizing the potential impact of words, James admonishes us: "Let everyone be quick to listen, *slow to speak* (Jas 1:19).

Verbal truthfulness is about saying things in the right way. But what is the right way? The right way is with love (cf. Eph 4:15). Communication takes place on two levels.[15] At one layer, the speaker is simply conveying information to the listener. This is called content. However, the second level—the relational level—expresses the amount of care, responsiveness, and power that exists between the two people engaged in the conversation. Without love, the conversation is prone to going awry.

Truthfulness is about conveying information in the right way—with love. The truthful person pays attention not only to the content of the message but also to the impact of the words. Honesty is never an excuse for being cruel or unkind. Truthful people are carefully attuned to how the listener is receiving their words. If their words are being hurtful, they may decide to proceed more slowly or wait until a better time to communicate their message.

The Right Purpose

Words serve a purpose. Because of the relational level of communication, our words always have a relational purpose. So, what is that purpose? Jesus provides the answer when he says,

"The truth will make you free" (John 8:32).

Freedom is complex. For some people, freedom simply means having the ability to choose.[16] According to this view, whether the choice is good or bad is inconsequential, because being free to choose is all that really matters. Yet having the ability to choose is only one aspect of freedom. Real freedom has another side. People are truly free when they can choose that which is truly good for them. Truth sets the listener free when the communication enables the listener to do that which is best for him or her.

Consider the case of Jeron and Alisha. Jeron has spent too much on a purchase, and now he feels he doesn't have enough money to go out on a date. Jeron is in a pickle. On the one hand, he is ashamed of his financial blunder. Additionally, he wants Alisha to think well of him, but he is afraid that she is going to get mad at him. As a result, he could say to Alisha, "I've had had a lot of unexpected bills this month, so I am afraid I need to cancel our date for Saturday." On the other hand, if he wants the truth to set her free, he will give her all the information and invite her into the conversation. As a result, she can speak her mind and convey what she thinks is best for her.

Truthful Listening

Truthfulness does not simply apply to the speaker. We also need to be truthful listeners. Communication is a reciprocal process. One person speaks while the other one listens. According to Adam McHugh, the word, "listen," appears in the Bible over fifteen hundred times.[17] Without a good listener, effective communication is impossible. For the speaker's message to be accurately understood, the listener must employ certain skills: attending, accepting, clarifying, and so on. Truthfulness is not only about what we say; it also pertains to the way we listen.

Centered Living

How can we extend the gentle activities of Centering Prayer into our ordinary lives? That is the question we have been considering in this section of each chapter. Which practices have we touched on in this chapter that are relevant to our communication with people who are close, distant, and in-between? Our response to this practical question takes us into Centered Living.

Here, I will turn to the findings of Andrew Newberg and Mark Waldman.[18] They present three claims arising from neuroscience that complement what we have learned in this chapter. The three strategies they spell out for enhancing the dynamics of our conversations are: to cultivate silence, to listen deeply, and to speak slowly.

Newberg and Waldman's findings bolster an idea that is foundational to Centering Prayer—that *cultivating silence* is the best ground for producing the words we speak. Words are more effective and powerful when they arise from silence. Silence is a strategy that prepares us for conversations with family members, friends, and neighbors.

A second principle of contemplation supported by Newberg and Waldman's research is the need to *listen deeply*. The way we listen to others makes a huge difference to our conversations. Bioethicist Stephen Post and science journalist Jill Neimark say three things about listening that remind me of contemplative prayer.[19] First, listening is about pausing and attending. Second, when we listen, we are allowing ourselves to be still and to be present. Finally, listening entails sitting down and waiting. When someone listens deeply to us and when we return the favor, something amazing happens. At the end of a day when we have engaged in deep listening, we can assert: "Today I trusted someone. Today someone trusted me. Today I was able to give something significant to another."[20]

The final strategy offered by Newberg and Waldman is to *speak slowly*. We have noted that this finding resonates with the Letter of James, who was teaching us to avoid knee-jerk verbal responses in our interactions with others. Instead of replying impulsively, we need to pause and think carefully before firing off a barrage of words. Newberg and Waldman are getting at the same thing. They claim that "the true power of speaking slowly is in the increased consciousness it brings."[21] Bringing awareness to the pace at which we speak also shines a light on the words and message that we are communicating.

Slow speech by the speaker impacts the listener. First, speaking with an unhurried voice has a calming effect on the person hearing the message. Second, reducing your rate of speech increases the listener's ability to comprehend what you are saying. This final suggestion—speaking slowly—is one that I employ regularly as a counselor. As I consciously slow the rate of my speech, I see my clients begin to relax and witness their increased ability to absorb my message. Sometimes going leisurely helps us get there—to better relationships—faster.

Conclusion

Communication is vital in our relationships with others, whether human or divine. Through the lens of Centering Prayer, we have explored essential elements of good conversations—

cultivating silence, listening carefully, being gentle with our words, and speaking with good intentions. We have integrated ancient contemplative principles with modern findings from neuroscience. We have observed how contemplative-based strategies bring us to the virtue of truthfulness.

One final observation about truthfulness is that truthfulness takes courage. It takes *courage*, in the middle of a conversation, to choose words that convey our view accurately; it takes courage to be honest even if doing so exposes our weaknesses and shortcomings; and it takes courage to speak the truth in love.

Early pioneers in positive psychology Martin Seligman and Christopher Peterson noticed the link between truthfulness and courage.[22] They even viewed truthfulness as a route or means to courage. Making a similar observation, Paul Wadell observed, "Without the courage to speak the truth to one another in love, and the courage to allow others to speak truthfully to us, we inevitably grow distant and apart."[23] Our relationships depend upon truthfulness and good communications.

JUSTICE

The day I received my doctorate in counselor education was a happy occasion. I had completed all the required courses and the internships had provided me with the necessary clinical hours and supervision that I needed for licensure. I had even completed a dissertation on a counseling protocol for couples going through divorce.

Despite the pressure and stress, I enjoyed being a student —studying new ideas, practicing in the counseling center, and even doing research. However, getting a degree in counselor education was not an end in itself. Instead, it was preparing me for something else. It was setting the groundwork for teaching students and offering counseling to clients. Graduate school was preparation for my work in the real world.

We are mistaken when we think of Centering Prayer as our end point. Centering Prayer is not just a journey inward, it is also preparation for a journey outward. In Centering Prayer, we are integrating silence and action.

Centering Prayer

Contemplative prayer can be jarring, because it brings us face-to-face with the human condition. The truth is that we are all ill. Our disease is a deep, felt sense of alienation from God, others, and our self. Even as children, we feel this acute pain and attempt to cope with it by unconsciously developing a system for creating our own happiness.[1] Within the contemplative tradition, this disease is typically referred to as the false self.

You will recall that the false self is the sense that our identity is tied to what we do, what we have, and what others think of us.[2] We wind up pursuing these things in search of happiness. The problem is that this path takes us in the wrong direction. Instead of producing joy and delight, the false self brings unhappiness.

Our Vulnerable Condition

The truth is that we are all fundamentally the same. We are vulnerable because we are susceptible to being hurt. We are harmed because we are looking in the wrong direction for happiness. We experience pain because our lives are driven by values—doing, having, and being recognized—that don't satisfy.

To one degree or another, we react with self-judgment and self-contempt to our own inability to produce happiness. These emotional reactions culminate in a feeling of shame—the sense that there is something terribly wrong with me for falling short of the ideal person I want to portray. Shame is connected to the feeling that I am defective and weak as opposed to powerful and successful.

Centering Prayer as Healing

Centering Prayer transforms and heals our wounds. There are two ways in which contemplative prayer transforms and mends our lives. First, healing comes through *self-knowledge*.

Thomas Keating maintains that "it takes courage to face up to the process of self-knowledge, but it is the only way of getting in touch with our true identity and ultimately with our true Self."[3] This is where we acknowledge who we are. We admit to God, who loves us, that we are driven by the motives to do more, have more, and gain more recognition.

The second source of healing is *self-acceptance*. In Centering Prayer, we learn not only to accept our thoughts but also to accept ourselves. This favorable self-regard is not dependent upon change, modification, or goodness. We don't wait until we reach some point of self-improvement to offer ourselves acceptance. Instead, we receive our thoughts, our emotions, and ourselves just as they are now. Centering Prayer gives us the opportunity to be alone with Jesus and to ponder the reality of who we are, face our places of pain, and gradually befriend our weaknesses.

How do we become a friend to our weakness? What is the origin of this kind of self-acceptance? Thomas Keating suggests two sources. The first is through the silence of Centering Prayer. He notes that "as you experience the reassurance that comes from interior silence, you have more courage to face the dark side of your personality and to accept yourself as you are."[4]

The second source is the experience of being in God's love and presence. As we Center, we encounter the love of God. As we sit in silence, at our core, we come to know that we are loved by God. Keating notes that "there is nothing more affirming, in fact, than the experience of God's presence. That revelation says . . . 'You are a good person. I created you and I love you.'"[5] This love of God "heals the negative feelings we have about ourselves."[6] Indeed, it is our exposure to God's love that enables us to accept ourselves.

From Silence to Action

Contemplation is a transforming interior journey. As we sit in silence, we face our vulnerable parts and enjoy the self-acceptance that emerges from the experience of God's love and presence. However, contemplative prayer doesn't stop there. It is preparing us for another type of journey; it is "a preparation for action."[7] In fact, the purpose of this prayer, as Keating notes, "is not more prayer or silence, but the integration of prayer and silence with activity."[8]

Richard Rohr describes this action as "a radical journey outward."[9] In agreement with Keating, he notes that "the effect of contemplation is authentic action, and if contemplation doesn't lead to genuine action, then it remains only self-preoccupation."[10] Centering Prayer is designed to propel us from interior silence to exterior action. Such action is an outward journey that is expressed through a "commitment to the social issues of our time."[11]

The Virtue of Justice

When we connect the inward journey with the outward journey, we are drawing a straight line from contemplative prayer to character. The virtue that drives us into the social issues of our time is called justice. Timothy Keller maintains that "if you are trying to live a life in accordance with the Bible, the concept and call to justice are inescapable."[12] Let us now consider how this concept and call to justice relates to Centering Prayer.

Justice as Seeing

According to Stanley Hauerwas, "Justice is a way of seeing."[13] There are three elements to this way of seeing. First, justice

means that we view people as *vulnerable*. Contemplative prayer reveals that we are all exposed to harm. Certain members of society, however, are particularly susceptible to injury and damage.

When Old Testament writers wrote about justice, they focused on the lowly ones, the vulnerable ones.[14] These authors used a hierarchical image: some people were at the top of the social ladder, while others were at the bottom. Four groups of downtrodden people are continually mentioned in the Old Testament: widows, orphans, immigrants, and the poor. These groups were without social and economic resources of their own. Therefore, justice was about defending and protecting these lowly ones, the ones without power.

Jesus expands our concept of the downtrodden beyond these four groups of people. He includes people who are vulnerable for other reasons and in other ways. Jesus admonishes us to care for the hungry, the stranger, the naked, the sick, and the imprisoned (cf. Matt 25:35–36). Jesus teaches us to care for the poor, the crippled, the lame, and the blind (cf. Luke 14:13).

Second, justice means seeing people as being *worthy*.[15] Justice is about honoring and respecting the other person's significance and value and regarding all humans as having equal dignity. What are the grounds for the importance of every individual? Human dignity is rooted in the love of God. God's love imparts to us the worth that we would otherwise not have. In Centering Prayer, God's love is essential in our quest for self-acceptance.

Third, justice means viewing others as having inherent *rights*. In other words, to value an individual's worth means observing and respecting their rights. Valuing the marginalized person's worth motivates us to protect and defend their rights—that is, the right to food, clothing, health care, shelter, and visitation (cf. Matthew 25:35, 36).

The Face of Injustice

The face of injustice emerges when we view certain individuals in our society as worthless and become blind to their value. We begin by disrespecting the downtrodden, by demeaning, insulting, or belittling them. Next, we deprive them of their rights and convince ourselves that they don't deserve to be treated with basic human dignity. This leads to actions that devalue our brothers and sisters and sends the message, "I count and you do not, and I may thus use you as a mere thing."[16]

Justice as Action

Both the Old and New Testament writers call us to act justly, that is, to move from injustice to justice (cf. Micah 6:8). This is clearly a call to action. Justice is about behavior, and Jesus, as we have noted, supports this view when he instructs us to feed the hungry, clothe the naked, welcome the stranger, look after the sick, and visit the prisoner (cf. Matt 25:35, 36). The Letter of James reminds us, "If a brother or sister is naked and lacks daily food, and one of you says to them, 'Go in peace; keep warm and eat your fill,' and yet you do not supply their bodily needs, what is the good of that?" (Jas 2:15, 16).

Justice calls us to get personally involved with the poor and forgotten in our society. The just person observes that the fabric of our society is torn and that certain members are falling through. Keller writes, "The only way to reweave and strengthen the fabric is by weaving yourself into it."[17] The outward journey of justice invites the just person off the sidelines and into the game, into involvement with the marginalized groups of our society. We cannot send someone else in our place. We must put ourselves directly in the process of caring for the lowly in our world. In fact, Nicholas Wolterstorff maintains that "you cannot be Christian without a concern for the poor, the oppressed, the down-trodden."[18]

Let us conclude by returning to a parable we discussed in the first chapter—the parable of the good Samaritan (Luke 10:30–36). In this parable, Jesus reveals the character of a good neighbor, but I would add that the Samaritan was also a man of justice. Justice is present in how he views the injured man. The passage says of the Samaritan that "when he *saw him*, he was moved with pity" (v. 33). I believe the Samaritan *saw him* as *vulnerable*, as a person of *worth*, and as a person with *inherent rights*. Second, justice reveals itself in action. Jesus gives a detailed account of how the Samaritan cares for the injured man by bandaging his wounds, putting him on his own donkey, taking him to an inn, and paying for his lodging (cf. vv. 34, 35). Because he is a just man, the Samaritan is concerned for a complete stranger. He gives of his time, his skill, and his money. He gets personally involved.

Centered Living

The inward journey of Centering Prayer has a profound impact on how we live our daily lives. Centering Prayer is not just about silence; it propels us into action. Earlier in this chapter, we examined how Centering Prayer leads us toward remediating the injustices of our time. Contemplative prayer causes us to get personally involved with members of our society who have been unjustly harmed and injured.

But, what about those times when we ourselves are the victims of mistreatment and injustice? How do we respond? Do the principles of Centering Prayer assist us in such a situation? Both psychology and the contemplative tradition provide a similar response to this question: forgiveness. Let us now consider what forgiveness means in practical terms.

The Need for Forgiveness

We have all been wounded and will be wounded in the future by others, whether through rejection and betrayal or ridicule and humiliation. In some cases, our deepest hurts may have come as a result of unjust treatment and abuse.

How do we respond to such hurts? In some instances, we may have excused the injurer or tried to convince ourselves that the offense didn't happen. At other times, we might blame ourselves for the injury or we might be determined to seek revenge. From the viewpoint of psychology, these responses don't help us heal from the wounds of injustice.[19]

The Process of Forgiveness

Forgiveness is a process that begins when we admit that we have suffered at the hands of others. Yes, we are vulnerable and susceptible to harm. According to co-developer of Centering Prayer, William Meninger, we must face the mistreatment we have endured and the consequences of that hurt.[20] In order to forgive, we must make a clear account of our injuries. What are my wounds? Who inflicted them? What specifically needs to be healed? In Centering Prayer, we have learned that healing comes through *self-knowledge* and that it takes courage to face and accept our pain.

After admitting our wounds and recognizing who inflicted them, we move to the next step—*acceptance*. We accept the reality of our hurt and admit our past and the pain that the injury caused.

For many of us, this acceptance is accompanied by *anger*, but it is a good and positive kind of anger. It is an anger that says, "I will not allow this to happen again." This kind of anger is a sign that we are not helpless. Embedded in the anger is our refusal to be the victim of such abuse or mistreatment again.

Forgiveness is a process that takes place over time. When we face our past, when we accept our hurts, when we angrily declare our refusal to be defined by our suffering, we are ready to move forward. Now, our wounds begin to heal. This is when forgiveness takes place, because forgiveness is the natural by-product of healing. Meninger observes: "Forgiveness is not something we do directly but is something that happens to us. When we allow this healing to take place, we will discover that forgiveness has also taken place."[21]

Signs of Forgiveness

There are specific indicators that forgiveness is taking place. Our task is less about making things happen and more about noticing that they have already taken place. The signs of forgiveness involve changes in our thoughts, emotions, and behavior. For example, as a result of forgiveness, we have stopped replaying thoughts about the transgression and transgressor. Letting go of old thoughts allows us to release the painful emotions that accompany the old ruminations. We stop seeking revenge and are no longer caught up in expressing anger about the transgression and transgressor. We are not expecting the injurer to do something for us. Of course, we have not forgotten the injury, but we are ready to move on.

This step of moving on can be compared to the process of moving outward. Once you have experienced healing on the inside, it is time to make external changes in your life. You are doing new things for yourself, such as improving your health, pursuing some interest or passion, or engaging in a new adventure. You are not only doing significant things for yourself, but offering other people your love and kindness.

Conclusion

We are vulnerable and we do experience pain in our lives. But, healing the deep wounds in our lives is possible. In this chapter, we have explored several means of recovery. Through the reassurance of interior silence, Centering Prayer makes restoration possible. Taking this inward journey prepares us for an outward one that includes the actions of justice and forgiveness.

15

KINDNESS AND GENTLENESS

At its core, Centering Prayer relates to how we handle our thoughts. When we respond appropriately to the images and feelings that enter our minds, we are more adequately prepared for the gift of God's presence. However, untrained reactions to mental activity can erect barriers to this contemplative experience. The important question is: Will I deal with my thoughts in a harsh or gentle manner? I must admit that far too often I have responded to unwanted notions and distractions with rejection. But that is not the way of Centering Prayer.

Centering Prayer and Gentleness

A basic principle of Centering Prayer is handling our thoughts with gentleness. In his guidelines for Centering Prayer, Keating suggests that "when you become aware of thoughts, return ever-so-gently to the sacred word."[1] Here, Keating shines a bright light on the centrality and frequency of kindness within the practice of contemplative prayer. Every time we notice a thought, we are to practice kindness. Instead of meeting thoughts with judgment, such as, "That's a terrible idea," or "You are so bad at controlling your thoughts," we can greet them with acceptance.

In Centering Prayer, we are often confronted with an endless line of thoughts. One after the other, they compete for our attention. In my case, during twenty minutes of prayer, interior silence can sometimes be hard to find. I am encouraged to know that each distraction offers me another opportunity to practice and extend gentleness to myself.

Centering Prayer clearly involves activity. As we have already noted, this method of prayer is not about doing nothing. Instead, we are regularly engaged in the actions of letting go of our thoughts and returning to the sacred word. In Centering Prayer, we are not advised to do these things in any manner we desire. Instead, we are instructed to carry out two simple acts— *letting go* and *returning to the sacred word*—with gentleness.

Multiplicity of Selves

Centering prayer brings to the surface a host of internal thoughts. For example, one thought might involve enumerating the list of tasks I must complete that day; another might remind me of how I have been selfish with my money; and yet another thought may express fear of what my boss thinks of me.

Some of these thoughts may be familiar, common, and close. But then there are the uncommon ideas and the whims that sneak into our mind, the ones that are unfamiliar and new. When we are unacquainted with these thoughts, we may get caught off-guard. Where do these frequent and unfamiliar thoughts originate?

The truth, which Centering Prayer reveals, is that we are not one self. Instead, there are many selves within us. As John O'Donohue notes, "Often it seems as if there is a crowd within the individual heart. Deep within, there is a gallery of different selves. There is a multiplicity of selves we encounter in our most inward meditations."[2]

Meeting these different selves during our times of silent prayer can be awkward and disturbing. As they appear, they may not fit so nicely with the strong, successful, and virtuous view of ourselves that we have so carefully constructed. Instead, we encounter those parts that are weak, frail, and wounded.

Centering Prayer confronts us with our own *otherness*. O'Donohue defines otherness as everything that is other than *you*.[3] (Here, the word "you" refers to the carefully constructed image of ourselves that we present to the world.) In contemplative prayer, we discover those unknown parts of ourselves that were previously hidden. They may seem strange, opposed to, and totally different from the way we present ourselves to the world. This experience of otherness within ourselves can be both embarrassing and alarming.

How will you respond to the abandoned, negative, and unwanted parts of yourself that you find hidden within? According to Henri Nouwen, this question leads us to the heart of our spiritual struggle.[4] Will you reject, loathe, and judge these marginalized parts of yourself or will you practice inner hospitality—welcoming them into a more complex and integrated definition of yourself?

When you demonstrate this type of hospitality, you are practicing gentleness or kindness. Speaking of our neglected selves, O'Donohue observes that "one of our sacred duties is to exercise kindness to them."[5] I am comforted by the truth that kindness is not intended just for family members, friends, and strangers. Instead, it is a virtue designed to help me interact with the weak and frail parts of myself. As Daniel Siegel writes, "Kindness is a way of honoring one's vulnerabilities."[6]

How do we practice gentleness or kindness during our time of silent prayer? We exercise gentleness by extending hospitality to all the thoughts that appear. None are treated with contempt or blame. No thoughts or feelings are made to feel detestable or judged. Instead, as Keating teaches us, one lets go of the thoughts as "one gently places the sacred word in one's awareness."[7]

Gentleness and Rest

Jesus enlarges our understanding of gentleness by combining it with the concept of *rest*. Jesus says, "Come to me, all you that are weary and are carrying heavy burdens, and I will give you *rest*. Take my yoke upon you, and learn from me; for I am *gentle* and humble in heart, and you will find *rest* for your souls" (Matt 11:28–29). In this passage, Jesus tells us that we find rest in the care of someone who is gentle.

Keating makes the concept of rest central to contemplative prayer. In one place he describes contemplation as resting in God: "Just rest in God's arms."[8]

Within the context of contemplative prayer, the impacts of gentleness and rest are immense. Something powerful happens to our mind and body when we experience interior silence along with the inner hospitality and rest that accompany it. A spark is ignited within that allows us to move from shame to self-acceptance, from fear to love. In fact, Keating observes that "the rest which comes about as a result of interior silence evokes the natural capacity of the human organism to throw off things that are harmful."[9] Furthermore, he adds that Centering Prayer "releases a dynamic" that can bring about the healing for which we so earnestly long.[10]

The Virtue of Kindness

Through our practice of Centering Prayer we may discover that our life is beginning to produce new fruit. In fact, one of the reasons we engage in Centering Prayer is "for the sake of its positive fruits in our life."[11] Indeed, one of the fruits of the Spirit that emerges from our Centering practice of gentleness is kindness.

Of course, here we can see that gentleness and kindness are not identical. Gentleness is the activity, whereas kindness is the fruit produced or derived from that activity. Let us now examine how the practice of gentleness contributes to developing the virtue of kindness.

Principles of Gentleness

Kindness stems from four principles of gentleness. First, gentleness is the act of attending to a need. The practice of Centering Prayer aims to focus on our most fundamental human requirement—to encounter the Divine Presence. However, we discover that thoughts create an obstacle to our focus. To be prepared for the gift of God's presence, we must learn how to let go of the feelings, ideas, and notions that demand our attention and return "ever-so-gently to the sacred word."

Second, a key to practicing gentleness is to know why you are being gentle with yourself. The only appropriate response is that you are exercising gentleness for the purpose of meeting the deepest longings of your heart: experiencing interior silence, being open to the Divine Presence, and knowing God in love.

Third, gentleness relies on trust. Centering Prayer confronts us with the question: Can I trust myself? Can I trust myself to be gentle when I become aware that my mind has wandered? In Centering Prayer, we are learning to respond with kindness to our own basic needs. We don't react with judgment or harshness to our passing thoughts. Instead, we extend gentleness to ourselves.

Finally, gentleness is a small action. Letting go of thoughts doesn't require a big show of emotions or activity. When we notice that we are engaged in thoughts, our response is small. We simply let go of the thought and "return ever-so-gently to the sacred word."

What is Kindness?

How do we describe kindness? Here, we will describe it by referring to the previously identified four principles of gentleness.

First, kindness is an action aimed at meeting the needs of others. Paul Wadell defines kindness as "the practice of charity by which we look for ways to do good for others."[12] Tara Cousineau states that "kindness is love in action. . . . It is an act of love that reflects genuine caring."[13] Virginia Held reminds us, caring (or kindness) is about attending to and fulfilling the wants of others.[14] It is about satisfying a need that the other person may not be able to meet by and/or for himself. When we see and hear the wants of someone and take responsibility for handling those needs, we are being kind.

Second, William Mattison observes that acts of kindness—if they are to be virtuous—must be carried out for the right reason.[15] If we do an apparently kind deed, but it is motivated by selfish interests, then the action has little to do with the virtue of kindness. Truly kind deeds must have the correct motive. The proper question behind kindness is: Why am I engaged in this action? When we are looking out for the interests of others instead of our own interests, we are exhibiting true kindness.

Third, kindness is characterized by trust. Think of those special people you trust. Why do you trust them? Because you can depend on them to respond in a caring way to your needs. And what happens when a person consistently and dependably shows up to fulfill your needs? You begin to trust them. As Virginia Held says, "Caring and trust sustain each other."[16]

Finally, kindness is the only virtue we think of as being doled out in small doses. For example, we often refer to "small acts of kindness." Caring consists of the small deeds we carry out in response to the needs of those around us. We might offer someone a smile, a kind word, or a helping hand. These tiny acts of kindness accumulate and eventually become something large and beautiful. As Stephen Post and Jill Neimark observe, "A life well lived is really the sum of thousands of small, ordinary acts of kindness."[17]

Centered Living

In Centering Prayer, we are gently leaving our thoughts behind and attending to the Divine, to the Spirit. In being faithful to this practice, Basil Pennington points out, "we will begin to function out of this divine sense even when we rise from the Prayer and go about our daily activity."[18] This profound change to the activity of our life is Centered Living.

In the same way that Centering Prayer is "first of all and above all, an interpersonal relationship"[19] with God, Centered Living focuses primarily on our relationships with others. How does the exercise of gentleness result in the fruit of kindness in the way we treat those who are both close to and distant from us?

Activating Kindness

Kindness is like a light switch that can be turned either on or off. To bring kindness to our interactions with others, we must notice the conditions that activate it. And, of course, we must be sensitive to times when kindness is absent. With this awareness, we can then take appropriate steps to respond with care.

Science informs us that kindness can be switched off by what is called the "threat response system." When we are afraid or overwhelmed with busyness, exhaustion, and overwork, the threat response system can be easily stimulated. When this happens, we automatically shift into a self-protective mode. Instead of moving toward friends and family, we reactively move away from or against them, and concern and care change to indifference and apathy. A sensitive desire to attend to the needs of others turns to callousness and negativity. Cousineau notes that "when you are disillusioned, afraid, or feeling threatened or unsafe, it's hard to engage your kindness instinct."[20]

To turn kindness on, we are equipped with what science calls the "calm and connect system." When this routine comes "online," we experience an overall sense of well-being and consequently are primed to care about and focus on the interests of others. In other words, we become attuned to and desire to meet the needs of the people in our life.

Centering Prayer can activate our calm and connect system. Letting go of alarming thoughts, entering into interior silence, and being open to God's presence can have a profound calming effect. Being ever so gentle with ourselves as we sit with God in Centering Prayer can translate into kindness toward others as we move out into our daily life. Cousineau, identifying this effect, says that contemplative practices can "ignite our caring circuitry."[21]

Empathy, Kindness, and Centering Prayer

Without empathy, kindness to self and others is almost impossible. Empathy motivates kindness. What is empathy and how is it related to kindness and to Centering Prayer?

According to Cousineau, there are three aspects to empathy: emotional, behavioral, and intellectual.[22] The emotional aspect of empathy allows us to feel with our fellow human beings. With emotional empathy, we can actually feel the pain of others, especially when we directly experience or see another person suffering. This type of empathy motivates us to turn toward the needs of others in kindness.

The motivation to care for others activates the second aspect of empathy: the behavioral aspect. Here, we actually do something to meet the other person's needs. Instead of sitting idly by, we take appropriate action, and our behaviors are backed by the right reason. We are doing something for the other person's good. It is in their best interests, not our own.

The final aspect of empathy is intellectual. Empathy enables us to take on the perspective of the other person. When we are able to see things from the other person's point of view, they experience our interest in them. This small act of kindness—*perspective-taking*—lets others know that we are safe and trustworthy.

Empathy emerges from the exercise of gentleness, which is essential in the practice of Centering Prayer. In Centering Prayer, gentleness allows us to feel with the pain that we encounter as we sit with God. Gentleness motivates us to act with kindness toward self. Rather than responding with criticism or harshness, there is an ever-so-gentle returning to the sacred word.

Finally, in gentleness we acknowledge that letting go of thoughts is not easy. Having our attention captured by distracting feelings and ideas is normal and to be expected. We extend kindness to self by avoiding judgment. Our only response to a wandering mind is gentleness.

EPILOGUE

The purpose of this book has been to set you on a path of contemplative prayer. As we have continued in our journey, we have discovered that contemplative prayer is nothing but love, that is, love for God, others, and self. It is not an easy, smooth, and romantic approach to love. Instead, we have embraced all the different sides of love: suffering as well as joy, emotional pain as well as rest, and vulnerability as well as safety.

It is amazing how something as ordinary as repeatedly returning a wandering attention can produce love. Sharon Salzberg makes a similar point about the practice of mindfulness by pointing out that it is rich soil for the growth of real love.[1]

Centering Prayer is the practice of love, but not some form of love that gets described in only romantic or idyllic terms. Love can be calming, restful, and reassuring, but it can also be encountered in many other, unexpected ways. For me, love has found fertile ground to grow in contemplative prayer when I can't concentrate, when emotional junk appears, and when I get bored.

My pursuit of God's love in Centering Prayer is often not glamorous. I find God's love and presence in mundane and ordinary things like sitting still for twenty minutes, watching thoughts as they come and go, returning constantly to my sacred word, and then, starting all over again. For me, love is like sitting at my favorite cafe, waiting for God to show up—which God always does—realizing that I won't immediately recognize God's presence, but knowing that something good will take place because I have lingered for twenty minutes. Love is about simply showing up and saying, "Here I am."

The miraculous thing is that these simple actions of love—letting go of thoughts, being open to God, waiting without going away, paying attention, being gentle, and using a sacred word—begin to turn us into people of character. The virtues that we have explored in this book are all rooted in love. We can't be loving without patience, we can't be loving without compassion, we can't be loving without kindness, and so on.

As we grow in the virtues of love, we are taking on the character of Jesus. We are called to a character like that of God's—a character constituted of love. Paul Wadell asserts that "God is love. And we should be too. That's Christianity in a nutshell."[2]

Centered Living refers to the practical ways in which we bring love into our everyday life. Love is expressed in how we relate to God, others, and ourselves on a daily basis. We exhibit love in all of these relationships when we are sensitive to suffering, when we hope that things will get better, when we let go of our need to be right, and when we show curiosity. We are being loving when we listen, when we forget about ourselves, when we make good choices, and when we stick to the task.

You may have opened this book because you were interested in getting closer to God. Hopefully, this book has helped you in your pursuit of God's love, but I wish for you so much more. I pray that you have extended the borders of your love from God out to others and inward to yourself.

NOTES

Introduction

1. Brian D. McLaren, *Seeking Aliveness* (New York: Hachette Book Group, 2017), 291.

2. Thomas Merton, *New Seeds of Contemplation* (New York: New Directions Publishing Company, 1961), 1.

3. Thomas Keating, *Manifesting God* (New York: Lantern Books, 2005).

4. James Wilhoit, "Contemplative and Centering Prayer," in *Embracing Contemplation*, ed. J. H. Coe and K. C. Stroble (Downers Grove, IL: InterVarsity Press, 2019), 224–40.

5. Thomas Keating, *Open Mind, Open Heart* (New York: Continuum Publishing Co., 1999), 14.

6. Murdoch O' Madagain, *Centering Prayer and the Healing of the Unconscious* (New York: Lantern Books, 2007), 107.

7. Ibid., 71.

8. Thomas Merton, *Conjectures of a Guilty Bystander* (New York: Doubleday, 1966), 142.

9. Thomas Keating, *Open Mind, Open Heart* (New York: Continuum, 1999), 3.

10. Ibid., 114.

11. William James, *The Principles of Psychology* (Cambridge, MA: Harvard University Press, 1890/1981), 401.

12. Keating, *Open Mind, Open Heart*, 45.

Chapter 1: Compassion

1. Thomas Keating, *Open Mind, Open Heart* (New York: Continuum, 1999), 76.

2. Eleonore Stump, *Wandering in Darkness* (Oxford: Clarendon Press, 2012), 10, 11.

3. Ibid., 123.

4. Ibid., 156.

5. Keating, *Open Mind, Open Heart*, 77.

6. Paul J. Waddell, *Happiness and the Christian Moral Life*, 2nd ed. (New York: Rowman & Littlefield Publishers, Inc., 2012), 69.

7. Peter Kreeft, *Making Sense Out of Suffering* (Ann Arbor, MI: Servant Books, 1986).

8. Alasdair C. MacIntyre, *Dependent Rational Animals: Why Human Beings Need the Virtues* (Peru, IL: Open Court Publishing Company, 1999), 2.

9. Carolyn Whitney-Brown, *Jean Vanier: Essential Writings* (Maryknoll, NY: Orbis Books, 2008).

10. M. Basil Pennington, *Centered Living: The Way of Centering Prayer* (Liguori, MO: Liguori Publications, 1999), 32.

11. Robert C. Roberts, *Spiritual Emotions: A Psychology of Christian Virtues* (Grand Rapids, MI: William B. Eerdmans Publishing Co., 2007).

12. Peter Kreeft, *Three Philosophies of Life* (San Francisco, CA: Ignatius Press, 1989), 113.

Chapter 2: Courage

1. Thomas Keating, *Open Mind, Open Heart* (New York: Continuum, 1999), 14.

2. Ibid., 55.

3. We will discuss the use of a sacred word in more detail in Chapter 13.

4. Ibid., 44.

5. Ibid., 68.

6. Ibid., 45.

7. Ibid., 57.

8. John O'Donohue, *Walking in Wonder* (New York: Convergent Books, 2015), 56.

9. Dallas Willard, *The Spirit of the Disciplines* (New York: HarperCollins Publishers, 1988), 163.

10. Peter Kreeft, *Making Sense Out of Suffering* (Ann Arbor, MI: Servant Books, 1986), 11.

11. Brennan Manning, *Ruthless Trust* (New York: HarperCollins Publishers, 2000), 122.

12. Keating, *Open Mind, Open Heart*, 41.

13. Ibid., 96.

14. Rebecca K. DeYoung, *Glittering Vices* (Grand Rapids, MI: Brazos Press, 2009), 148.

15. Stanley Hauerwas, *The Character of Virtue* (Grand Rapids, MI: Wm. B. Eerdmans Publishing Company, 2018), 111.

16. Sue Johnson, *Love Sense* (New York: Little, Brown and Company, 2013).

Chapter 3: Virtuous Anger

1. Roy F. Baumeister, *The Cultural Animal* (New York: Oxford University Press, 2005), 196–203.

2. Ibid.

3. Thomas Keating, *Open Mind, Open Heart* (New York: Continuum, 1999), 69.

4. Martin Laird, *A Sunlit Absence* (New York: Oxford University Press, 2011), 14.

5. Gerald G. May, *The Awakened Heart* (New York: HarperCollins Publishers, 1991), 81.

6. Cynthia Bourgeault, *Centering Prayer and Inner Awakening* (Cambridge, MA: Cowley Publications, 2004).

7. Ibid., 143.

8. Ibid., 147.

9. Robert C. Roberts, "Temperance," in *Virtues and Their Vices*, ed. K. Timpe and C. A. Boyd (New York: Oxford University Press, 2014), 93–111.

10. Zac Cogley, "A Study of Virtuous and Vicious Anger," in *Virtues and Their Vices*, ed. K. Timpe and C. A. Boyd (New York: Oxford University Press, 2014), 199–214.

11. Thomas Keating, *Invitation to Love* (New York: Continuum, 2000), 131.

12. Rebecca K. DeYoung, *Glittering Vices* (Grand Rapids, MI: Brazos Press, 2009), 133.

Chapter 4: Hope

1. William C. Mattison, *The Sermon on the Mount and Moral Theology* (New York: Cambridge University Press. 2017), 226.

2. Thomas Keating, *Open Mind, Open Heart* (New York: Continuum, 1999), 34.

3. Stanley Hauerwas, *The Character of Virtue* (Grand Rapids, MI: Wm. B. Eerdmans Publishing Company. 2018), 95.

4. Peter Atterton, Matthew Calarco, and Maurice Friedman, *Levinas and Buber: Dialogue and Difference* (Pittsburgh, PA: Duquesne University Press, 2004), 51.

5. Keating, *Open Mind, Open Heart*, 74.

6. William C. Mattison, *Introducing Moral Theology: True Happiness and the Virtues* (Grand Rapids, MI: Brazos Press. 2008), 251.

7. Keating, *Open Mind, Open Heart*, 76.

8. Ibid., 36.

9. Gordon Hempton, *One Square Inch of Silence* (New York: Free Press, 2009), 6.

10. M. Basil Pennington, *Centered Living: The Way of Centering Prayer* (Liguori, MO: Liguori Publications, 1999), 177.

11. Mark R. McMinn, *The Science of Virtue* (Grand Rapids, MI: Brazos Press. 2017), 121–22.

12. John M. Gottman, *The Science of Trust* (New York: W. W. Norton & Company, 2011).

Chapter 5: Gratitude

1. Thomas Keating, *Open Mind, Open Heart* (New York: Continuum, 1999), 71.

2. Ibid., 4.

3. Ibid., 71.

4. Ibid.

5. Ibid., 5.

6. Ibid., 88.

7. Ibid., 51.

8. Robert A. Emmons and Anjali Mishra, "Gratitude," in *Religion, Spirituality, and Positive Psychology*, ed. T. G. Plante (Santa Barbara, CA: Praeger, 2012), 9–29.

9. Robert C. Roberts, *Spiritual Emotions: A Psychology of Christian Virtues* (Grand Rapids, MI: William B. Eerdmans Publishing Co., 2007)131.

10. Robert A. Emmons, *Gratitude Works* (San Francisco, CA: Jossey-Bass, 2013).

11. Emmons and Mishra, "Gratitude," 9–29.

12. Ibid.

13. Ibid.

14. Russ Harris, *ACT with Love* (Oakland, CA: New Harbinger Publications, Inc., 2009).

15. Emmons, *Gratitude Works*, 30.

16. Ibid.

17. Shane J. Lopez, Jennifer T. Pedrottie, and C. R. Snyder, *Positive Psychology: The Scientific and Practical Exploration of Human Strengths*, 4th ed. (Thousand Oaks, CA: SAGE Publications, Inc., 2019).

Chapter 6: Humility

1. M. Basil Pennington, *True Self/False Self* (New York, The Crossroad Publishing Co., 2000), 33–34.

2. Ibid., 37.

3. Thomas Keating, *Open Mind, Open Heart* (New York: Continuum, 1999), 16.

4. Ibid., 68.

5. Roy F. Baumeister, "Emergence of Personhood: Lessons from Self and Identity," in *The Emergence of Personhood*, ed. M. Jeeves (Grand Rapids, MI: William B. Eerdmans Publishing Co., 2015), 68–83.

6. Keating, *Open Mind, Open Heart*, 102.

7. Ibid., 103.

8. Ibid., 13.

9. M. Basil Pennington, *Centering Prayer* (New York: Doubleday, 2001), 89.

10. Keating, *Open Mind, Open Heart*, 71.

11. Ibid., 59–60.

12. Ibid., 72.

13. Ibid.

14. Ibid., 114.

15. Peter Kreeft, *Back to Virtue* (San Francisco, CA: Ignatius Press, 1992), 99.

16. Craig A. Boyd, "Pride and Humility: Tempering the Drive for Excellence," in *Virtues and Their Vices*, ed. K. Timpe and C. A. Boyd (New York: Oxford University Press, 2014), 245–66.

17. Everett L. Worthington and Scott T. Allison, *Heroic Humility* (Washington, DC: American Psychological Association, 2018).

18. Ibid., 59.

19. Kreeft, *Back to Virtue*, 100.

20. Keating, *Open Mind, Open Heart*, 64.

21. Leslie S. Greenberg and Rhonda N. Goldman, *Emotion-Focused Couples Therapy* (Washington, DC: American Psychological Association, 2013)

Chapter 7: Trust

1. Thomas Merton, *New Seeds of Contemplation* (New York: New Directions Publishing Corporation, 1972), 126.

2. Thomas Keating, *Open Mind, Open Heart* (New York: Continuum, 1999), 51.

3. Ibid., 72.

4. Peter Kreeft, *Back to Virtue* (San Francisco, CA: Ignatius Press, 1992), 74. (Italics in the original.)

5. Ibid.

6. Keating, *Open Mind, Open Heart*, 100.

7. Ibid., 72.

8. Merton, *New Seeds of Contemplation*, 127–28.

9. Keating, *Open Mind, Open Heart*, 96.

10. Ibid., 36.

11. James R. Beck and Bruce Demarest, *The Human Person in Theology and Psychology* (Grand Rapids, MI: Kregel Publications, 2005), 136.

12. Gerald C. May, *The Awakened Heart* (New York: HarperCollins Publishers, 1991), 199.

13. Robert Audi, "Faith as an Attitude, Trait, and Virtue," in *Virtues and Their Vices*, ed. K. Timpe and C. A. Boyd (New York: Oxford University Press, 2014), 327–47.

14. Linda Zagzebski, "Trust," in *Virtues and Their Vices*, ed. K. Timpe and C. A. Boyd (New York: Oxford University Press, 2014), 269–83.

15. John M. Gottman, *The Science of Trust* (New York: W. W. Norton & Company, 2011), 43.

16. Susan M. Johnson, *Attachment Theory in Practice* (New York, The Guilford Press, 2019), 7.

17. Daniel J. Siegel, *The Mindful Therapist* (New York: W. W. Norton & Company, 2010), 75.

18. Ibid.

19. Gottman, *The Science of Trust*, 139.

20. Siegel, *The Mindful Therapist*, 74.

21. Gottman, *The Science of Trust*, 43.

22. Siegel, *The Mindful Therapist*, 76.

23. Ibid.

Chapter 8: Attentiveness

1. Richard Foster, *Prayer* (New York: HarperCollins Publishers, 1992), 158.

2. Paul J. Wadell, *Happiness and the Christian Moral Life*, 2nd ed. (New York: Rowman & Littlefield Publishers, Inc., 2012), 182.

3. Thomas Keating, *Open Mind, Open Heart* (New York: Continuum, 1999), 51.

4. Ibid., 15.

5. Daniel J. Siegel, *Aware: The Science and Practice of Presence* (New York: Penguin Random House LLC, 2018), 53.

6. Ibid., 56.

7. Keating, *Open Mind, Open Heart*, 95.

8. Ibid., 34.

9. Ibid., 94.

10. Siegel, *Aware*, 50.

11. William James, *The Principles of Psychology* (Cambridge, MA: Harvard University Press, 1890/1981), 401.

12. Jason S. Baehr, *Cultivating Good Minds: A Philosophical and Practical Guide to Educating for Intellectual Virtues*, www.intellectualvirtues.org., 2015.

13. Keating, *Open Mind, Open Heart*, 40.

14. Baehr, *Cultivating Good Minds*.

15. Alice Calaprice, *The Ultimate Quotable Einstein* (Princeton, NJ: Princeton University Press, 2013), 20.

16. Keating, *Open Mind, Open Heart*, 114.

17. Susan Johnson, *Love Sense* (New York: Little, Brown and Company. 2013), 91.

18. Simone Weil, *Waiting for God* (New York: HarperCollins Publishers, 2009), 64.

19. Paul J. Wadell, *Friendship and the Moral Life* (Notre Dame, IN: University of Notre Dame Press, 1989).

20. Rowan Williams, *Being Human* (Grand Rapids, MI: Wm. B. Eerdmans Publishing Co, 2018), 45.

21. Mary Gordon, *The Company of Women* (New York: Ballantine Books, 1980), 275.

22. Weil, *Waiting for God*, 65.

23. bid., 64.

24. Stephen Post and Jill Neimark, *Why Good Things Happen to Good People* (New York: Broadway Books, 2007), 232.

25. Siegel, *Aware*, 46–49.

26. Jason S. Baehr, *Cultivating Good Minds*.

Chapter 9: Open-Mindedness

1. Thomas Keating, *Open Mind, Open Heart* (New York: Continuum, 1999), 39.

2. Ibid., 37.

3. Ibid., 114.

4. Daniel J. Siegel, *The Mindful Therapist* (New York: W. W. Norton & Company, 2010), 103.

5. Keating, *Open Mind, Open Heart*, 74.

6. Ibid., 34.

7. Ibid., 109.

8. Robert C. Roberts and Jay Wood, *Intellectual Virtues* (New York: Oxford University Press, 2009).

9. Ibid., 210.

10. Keating, *Open Mind, Open Heart*, 64.

11. Paul J. Waddell, *Happiness and the Christian Moral Life*, 2nd ed. (New York: Rowman & Littlefield Publishers, Inc., 2012), 30.

12. Siegel, *The Mindful Therapist*, 103.

13. Ibid., 108.

14. Russ Harris, *ACT with Love* (Oakland, CA: New Harbinger Publications, Inc., 2009).

15. Keating, *Open Mind, Open Heart*, 56.

16. Ibid., 88.

17. Harris, *ACT with Love*, 54.

Chapter 10: Prudence

1. Thomas Keating, *Open Mind, Open Heart* (New York: Continuum, 1999), 39.

2. Ibid., 4.

3. Ibid., 47.

4. Bruce Demarest, *Satisfy Your Soul* (Colorado Springs, CO: NavPress, 1999), 164; cf. also Augustine, *Confessions*, Book 1 and Soliloquies 1.1.2.

5. Keating, *Open Mind, Open Heart*, 57.

6. Ibid., 36.

7. Ibid., 71.

8. Ibid., 47.

9. W. Jay Wood, "Prudence," in *Virtues and Their Vices*, ed. K. Timpe and C. A. Boyd (New York: Oxford University Press, 2014), 37–58.

10. William C. Mattison, *Introducing Moral Theology: True Happiness and the Virtues* (Grand Rapids, MI: Brazos Press, 2008).

11. Robert C. Roberts and Jay Wood, *Intellectual Virtues* (New York: Oxford University Press, 2009).

12. Paul J. Waddell, *Happiness and the Christian Moral Life*, 2nd ed. (New York: Rowman & Littlefield Publishers, Inc., 2012), 140.

13. Dallas Willard, *Renovation of the Heart* (Colorado Springs, CO: NavPress, 2012), 111.

14. Wood, "Prudence."

15. Louis Cozolino, *The Neuroscience of Human Relationships* (New York: W. W. Norton and Co., 2014), 98.

16. Pat Ogden and Janina Fisher, *Sensorimotor Psychotherapy* (New York: W. W. Norton and Co., 2015).

16. C. S. Lewis, *The Four Loves: An Exploration of the Nature of Love* (New York: Houghton Mifflin Harcourt Publishing Co., 1960), 61.

18. Mona Fishbane, *Loving With the Brain in Mind* (New York: W. W. Norton & Co., 2013).

19. Christian B. Miller, *The Character Gap* (New York: Oxford University Press, 2018).

20. Tim Muehlhoff and Todd V. Lewis, *Authentic Communication* (Downers Grove, IL: InterVarsity Press, 2010).

Chapter 11: Diligence

1. Thomas Keating, *Open Mind, Open Heart* (New York: Continuum, 1999), 45.

2. Gerald G. May, *The Awakened Heart* (New York: HarperCollins Publishers, 1991), 60.

3. David Frenette, *The Path of Centering Prayer* (Boulder, CO: Sounds True, Inc., 2012).

4. Keating, *Open Mind, Open Heart*, 40.

5. Ibid., 72.

6. Ibid., 36.

7. Ibid., 71.

8. Ibid.

9. Ibid., 45.

10. Phillip Cary, *Good News for Anxious Christians* (Grand Rapids, MI: Brazos Press, 2010).

11. Rebecca K. DeYoung, "Sloth: Some Historical Reflections on Laziness, Effort, and Resistance to the Demands of Love," in *Virtues and Their Vices*, ed. K. Timpe and C. A. Boyd (New York: Oxford University Press, 2014), 177–98.

12. Cf. Rebecca K. DeYoung, *Glittering Vices* (Grand Rapids, MI: Brazos Press, 2009).

13. Ibid., 79–98. See also Thomas Aquinas, *Summa Theologiae*, Q. 35.

14. Note that a talent was worth more than fifteen years' wages of a laborer.

15. Mona D. Fishbane, *Loving With the Brain in Mind* (New York: W. W. Norton & Co., 2013).

16. Nicholas Wolterstorff, *Justice in Love* (Grand Rapids, MI: Wm. B. Eerdmans Publishing Company, 2015), 90.

17. Rowan Williams, *Being Human: Bodies, Minds, Persons* (Grand Rapids, MI: Wm. B. Eerdmans Publishing Company, 2018).

18. Fishbane, *Loving With the Brain in Mind*.

Chapter 12: Patience

1. Thomas Keating, *Open Mind, Open Heart* (New York: Continuum, 1999), 40.

2. Ibid., 67.

3. Ibid.

4. Ibid., 72.

5. Ibid., 59.

6. Gerald G. May, *The Awakened Heart* (New York: HarperCollins Publishers, 1991), 48.

7. Keating, *Open Mind, Open Heart*, 55.

8. Stanley Hauerwas, *The Character of Virtue* (Grand Rapids, MI: William B. Eerdmans Publishing Company, 2018).

9. Tomas Halik, *Patience with God* (New York: Doubleday, 2009).

10. Christopher Peterson and Martin E. P. Seligman, *Character Strengths and Virtues* (New York: Oxford University Press, 2004).

11. Angela Duckworth, *Grit: The Power of Passion and Perseverance* (New York: Simon and Schuster, Inc., 2016).

Chapter 13: Truthfulness

1. Thomas Keating, *Open Mind, Open Heart* (New York: Continuum, 1999).

2. Ibid., 55.

3. Ibid., 44.

4. Ibid., 114.

5. Ibid., 71.

6. Ibid., 43.

7. Ibid., 57.

8. Richard Rohr, *What the Mystics Know* (New York: The Crossroad Publishing Company, 2015), 52.

9. Keating, *Open Mind, Open Heart*, 82.

10. Cf. Adam S. McHugh, *The Listening Life* (Downers Grove, IL: InterVarsity Press, 2015).

11. Stanley Hauerwas, *The Character of Virtue* (Grand Rapids, MI: Wm. B. Eerdmans Publishing Company, 2018), 58.

12. Ibid., 58.

13. Rohr, *What the Mystics Know*, 106.

14. Roy F. Baumeister, *The Cultural Animal* (New York: Oxford University Press, 2005), 178–244.

15. Tim Muehlhoff and Todd V. Lewis, *Authentic Communication* (Downers Grove, IL: InterVarsity Press, 2010).

16. William C. Mattison, *Introducing Moral Theology* (Grand Rapids, MI: Brazos Press, 2008).

17. McHugh, *The Listening Life.*

18. Andrew Newberg and Mark R. Waldman, *Words Can Change Your Brain* (New York: Hudson Street Press, 2012).

19. Stephen Post and Jill Neimark, *Why Good Things Happen to Good People* (New York: Broadway Books, 2007).

20. Ibid., 246.

21. Newberg and Waldman, *Words Can Change Your Brain*, 140.

22. Christopher Peterson and Martin E. P. Seligman, *Character Strengths and Virtues* (New York: Oxford University Press, 2004).

23. Paul J. Wadell, *Happiness and the Christian Moral Life*, 2nd ed. (New York: Rowman & Littlefield Publishers, Inc., 2012), 152.

Chapter 14: Justice

1. Thomas Keating, *Invitation to Love* (New York: Continuum, 2000), 130.

2. M. Basil Pennington, *True Self/False Self* (New York, The Crossroad Publishing Co., 2000), 37.

3. Thomas Keating, *Open Mind, Open Heart* (New York: Continuum, 1999), 96.

4. Ibid., 95.

5. Ibid., 66.

6. Ibid.

7. Ibid., 64.

8. Ibid., 65.

9. Richard Rohr, *What the Mystics Know* (New York: The Crossroad Publishing Company, 2015), 133.

10. Ibid., 121.

11. Ibid., 134.

12. Timothy Keller, *Generous Justice* (New York: Dutton, 2010), 18.

13. Stanley Hauerwas, *The Character of Virtue* (Grand Rapids, MI: Wm. B. Eerdmans Publishing Company, 2018), 103.

14. Nicholas Wolterstorff, *Justice: Rights and Wrongs* (Princeton, NJ: Princeton University Press, 2008).

15. Nicholas Wolterstorff, *Justice in Love* (Grand Rapids, MI: Wm. B. Eerdmans Publishing Company, 2015).

16. Jeffrie G. Murphy, *Getting Even* (New York: Oxford University Press, 2003), 77.

17. Keller, *Generous Justice*, 177.

18. Wolterstorff, *Justice: Rights and Wrongs*, 97.

19. Everett L. Worthington Jr. and Steven J. Sandage, *Forgiveness and Spirituality in Psychotherapy* (Washington, DC: American Psychological Association, 2016).

20. William A. Meninger, *The Process of Forgiveness* (New York: The Continuum Publishing Company, 2001).

21. Ibid., 37.

Chapter 15: Kindness and Gentleness

1. Thomas Keating, *Open Mind, Open Heart* (New York: Continuum, 1999), 139.

2. John O'Donohue, *Anam Cara* (New York: HarperCollins Publishers, Inc., 1997), 113.

3. John O'Donohue, *Walking in Wonder* (New York: Convergent Books, 2015).

4. Henri J. M. Nouwen, *The Return of the Prodigal Son* (New York: Image Books, 1994).

5. O'Donohue, *Anam Cara*, 17.

6. Daniel Siegel, *Mind* (New York: W. W. Norton & Company, 2017), 315.

7. Keating, *Open Mind, Open Heart*, 71.

8. Ibid., 89.

9. Ibid., 93.

10. Ibid., 99.

11. Ibid., 109.

12. Paul J. Wadell, "Charity: How Friendship with God Unfolds in Love for Others," in *Virtues and Their Vices*, ed. K. Timpe and C. A. Boyd (New York: Oxford University Press, 2014), 388.

13. Tara Cousineau, *The Kindness Cure* (Oakland, CA: New Harbinger Publications, Inc., 2018), 11.

14. Virginia Held, *The Ethics of Care* (New York: Oxford University Press, 2006).

15. William C. Mattison, *Introducing Moral Theology: True Happiness and the Virtues* (Grand Rapids, MI: Brazos Press, 2008).

16. Held, *The Ethics of Care*, 42.

17. Stephen Post and Jill Neimark, *Why Good Things Happen to Good People* (New York: Broadway Books, 2007), 12.

18. Basil M. Pennington, *Centered Living: The Way of Centering Prayer* (Liguori, MO: Liguori Publications, 1999), 32.

19. Ibid.

20. Cousineau, *The Kindness Cure*, 12.

21. Ibid., 107.

22. Ibid., 81.

Epilogue

1. Sharon Salzberg, *Real Love: The Art of Mindful Connection* (New York: Flatiron Books, 2017).

2. Paul J. Wadell, *Happiness and the Christian Moral Life*, 2nd ed. (New York: Rowman & Littlefield Publishers, Inc., 2012), 201.

BIBLIOGRAPHY

Atterton, Peter, Matthew Calarco, and Maurice Friedman. *Levinas and Buber: Dialogue and Difference*. Pittsburgh, PA: Duquesne University Press, 2004.

Audi, Robert. "Faith as Attitude, Trait, and Virtue." In *Virtues and Their Vices*, edited by Kevin Timpe and Craig A. Boyd, 327–48. New York: Oxford University Press, 2014.

Baehr, Jason S. *Cultivating Good Minds*; http://www.intellectualvirtues.org., 2015.

Baumeister, Roy F. *The Cultural Animal*. New York: Oxford University Press, 2005.

———. "Emergence of Personhood: Lessons From Self and Identity." In *The Emergence of Personhood: A Quantum Leap?* edited by Malcolm Jeeves, 68–86. Grand Rapids, MI: William B. Eerdmans Publishing Co., 2015.

Beck, James R., and Bruce Demarest. *The Human Person in Theology and Psychology*. Grand Rapids, MI: Kregel Publications, 2005.

Bourgeault, Cynthia. *Centering Prayer and Inner Awakening*. Cambridge, MA: Cowley Publications, 2004.

Boyd, Craig A. "Pride and Humility: Tempering the Drive for Excellence." In *Virtues and Their Vices*, edited by Kevin Timpe and Craig A. Boyd, 245–68. New York: Oxford University Press, 2014.

Calaprice, Alice. *The Quotable Einstein*. Princeton, NJ: Princeton University Press. 1996.

Cary, Phillip. *Good News for Anxious Christians*. Grand Rapids, MI: Brazos Press, 2010.

Cogley, Zac. "A Study of Virtuous and Vicious Anger." In *Virtues and Their Vices*, edited by Kevin Timpe and Craig A. Boyd, 199–224. New York: Oxford University Press, 2014.

Cousineau, Tara. *The Kindness Cure*. Oakland, CA: New Harbinger Publications, Inc., 2018.

Cozolino, Louis. *The Neuroscience of Human Relationships*. New York: W. W. Norton and Co., 2006.

Demarest, Bruce. *Satisfy Your Soul*. Colorado Springs, CO: NavPress, 1999.

DeYoung, Rebecca K. *Glittering Vices*. Grand Rapids, MI: Brazos Press, 2009.

———. "Sloth: Some Historical Reflections on Laziness, Effort, and Resistance to the Demands of Love." In *Virtues and Their Vices*, edited by Kevin Timpe and Craig A. Boyd, 177–98. New York: Oxford University Press, 2014.

Duckworth, Angela. *Grit: The Power of Passion and Perseverance*. New York: Simon and Schuster, Inc., 2016.

Emmons, Robert A., *Gratitude Works*. San Francisco, CA: Jossey-Bass, 2013.

Emmons, Robert A., and Anjali Mishra. "Gratitude." In *Religion, Spirituality, and Positive Psychology*, edited by Thomas G. Plante, 9–30. Santa Barbara, CA: Praeger, 2012.

Fishbane, Mona. *Loving with the Brain in Mind*. New York: W. W. Norton & Co. 2013.

Foster, Richard. Prayer. New York: HarperCollins Publishers, 1992.

Frenette, David. *The Path of Centering Prayer*. Boulder, CO: Sounds True, Inc., 2012.

Gordon, Mary. *The Company of Women*. New York: Ballantine Books, 1980.

Gottman, John M. *The Science of Trust*. New York: W. W. Norton & Company, 2011.

Greenberg, Leslie S., and Rhonda N. Goldman. *Emotion-Focused Couples Therapy*. Washington, DC: American Psychological Association, 2013.

Halik, Tomas. *Patience with God*. New York: Doubleday, 2009.

Harris, Russ. *ACT with Love*. Oakland, CA: New Harbinger Publications, Inc., 2009.

Hauerwas, Stanley, *The Character of Virtue*. Grand Rapids, MI: Wm. B. Eerdmans Publishing Company, 2018.

Held, Virginia. *The Ethics of Care*. New York: Oxford University Press, 2006.

Hempton, Gordon. *One Square Inch of Silence*. New York: Free Press, 2009.

James, William. *The Principles of Psychology*. Cambridge, MA: Harvard University Press, 1890/1981.

Johnson, Sue. *Attachment Theory in Practice*. New York, The Guilford Press, 2019.

———. *Love Sense*. New York: Little, Brown and Company, 2013.

Keating, Thomas. *Invitation to Love*. New York: Continuum, 2000.

———. *Manifesting God*. New York: Lantern Books, 2005.

———. *Open Mind, Open Heart*. New York: Continuum Publishing Co., 1999.

Keller, Timothy. *Generous Justice*. New York: Dutton, 2010.

Kreeft, Peter. *Back to Virtue*. San Francisco, CA: Ignatius Press, 1992.

———. *Making Sense Out of Suffering*. Ann Arbor, MI: Servant Books, 1986.

———. *Three Philosophies of Life*. San Francisco, CA: Ignatius Press, 1989.

Laird, Martin. *A Sunlit Absence*. New York: Oxford University Press, 2011.

Lewis, C. S. *The Four Loves: An Exploration of the Nature of Love*. New York: Houghton Mifflin Harcourt Publishing Co, 1960.

Lopez, Shane J., Jennifer T. Pedrottie, and C. R. Snyder. *Positive Psychology: The Scientific and Practical Exploration of Human Strengths*. 4th ed. Thousand Oaks, CA: SAGE Publications, Inc., 2019.

MacIntrye, Alasdair. *Dependent Rational Animals*. Peru, IL: Carus Publishing Company, 1999.

Manning, Brennan. *Ruthless Trust*. New York: HarperCollins Publishers, 2000.

Mattison, William C. *Introducing Moral Theology: True Happiness and the Virtues*. Grand Rapids, MI: Brazos Press. 2008.

———. *The Sermon on the Mount and Moral Theology*. New York: Cambridge University Press. 2017.

May, Gerald G. *The Awakened Heart*. New York: HarperCollins Publishers, 1991.

McHugh, Adam S. *The Listening Life*. Downers Grove, IL: InterVarsity Press, 2015.

McLaren, Brian D. *Seeking Aliveness*. New York: Hachette Book Group, 2017.

McMinn, Mark R. *The Science of Virtue*. Grand Rapids, MI: Brazos Press. 2017.

Meninger, William A. *The Process of Forgiveness*. New York: The Continuum Publishing Company, 2001.

Merton, Thomas. *Conjectures of a Guilty Bystander*. New York: Doubleday, 1966.

———. *New Seeds of Contemplation*. New York: New Directions Publishing Company, 1961.

Miller, Christian B. *The Character Gap*, New York: Oxford University Press, 2018.

Muehlhoff, Tim, and Todd V. Lewis. *Authentic Communication*. Downers Grove, IL: InterVarsity Press, 2010.

Murphy, Jeffrie G. *Getting Even*. New York: Oxford University Press, 2003.

Newberg, Andrew, and Mark R. Waldman. *Words Can Change Your Brain*. New York: Hudson Street Press, 2012.

Nouwen, Henri J. M. *The Return of the Prodigal Son*. New York: Image Books, 1994.

O'Donohue, John. *Anam Cara*. New York: HarperCollins Publishers, Inc., 1997.

———. *Walking in Wonder*. New York: Convergent Books, 2015.

Ogden, Pat, and Janina Fisher, *Sensorimotor Psychotherapy*. New York: W. W. Norton and Co., 2015.

O'Madagain, Murdoch. *Centering Prayer and the Healing of the Unconscious*. New York: Lantern Books, 2007.

Pennington, M. Basil. *Centered Living: The Way of Centering Prayer*. Liguori, MO: Liguori Publications, 1999.

———. *Centering Prayer*. New York: Doubleday, 2001.

———. *True Self/False Self*. New York, The Crossroad Publishing Co., 2000.

Peterson, Christopher, and Martin E. P. Seligman. *Character Strengths and Virtues*. New York: Oxford University Press, 2004.

Post, Stephen, and Jill Neimark. *Why Good Things Happen to Good People.* New York: Broadway Books, 2007.

Roberts, Robert C. *Spiritual Emotions: A Psychology of Christian Virtues.* Grand Rapids, MI: William B. Eerdmans Publishing Co., 2007.

———. "Temperance." In *Virtues and Their Vices*, edited by Kevin Timpe and Craig A. Boyd, 93–114. New York: Oxford University Press, 2014.

Roberts, Robert C., and Jay Wood. *Intellectual Virtues.* New York: Oxford University Press, 2009.

Rohr, Richard. *What the Mystics Know.* New York: The Crossroad Publishing Company, 2015.

Salzberg, Sharon. *Real Love: The Art of Mindful Connection.* New York: Flatiron Books, 2017.

Siegel, Daniel J. *Aware: The Science and Practice of Presence.* New York: Penguin Random House LLC, 2018.

———. *The Mindful Therapist.* New York: W. W. Norton & Company, 2010.

Stump, Eleonore. *Wandering in Darkness.* Oxford: Clarendon Press, 2012.

Wadell, Paul J. "Charity: How Friendship with God Unfolds in Love for Others." In *Virtues and Their Vices*, edited by Kevin Timpe and Craig A. Boyd, 369–92. New York: Oxford University Press, 2014.

———. *Friendship and the Moral Life.* Notre Dame, IN: University of Notre Dame Press, 1989.

———. *Happiness and the Christian Moral Life*, 2nd ed. New York: Rowman & Littlefield Publishers, Inc., 2012.

Weil, Simone. *Waiting for God.* New York: HarperCollins Publishers, 2009.

Wilhoit, James. "Contemplative and Centering Prayer." In *Embracing Contemplation: Reclaiming a Christian Spiri-*

tual Practice, edited by John H. Coe and Kyle C. Stroble, 224–40. Downers Grove, IL: InterVarsity Press, 2019.

Willard, Dallas. *Renovation of the Heart.* Colorado Springs, CO: NavPress, 2012.

———. *The Spirit of the Disciplines.* New York: Harper-Collins Publishers, 1988.

Williams, Rowan. *Being Human.* Grand Rapids, MI: Wm. B. Eerdmans Publishing Co, 2018.

Wolterstorff, Nicholas. *Justice in Love.* Grand Rapids, MI: Wm. B. Eerdmans Publishing Company, 2015.

———. *Justice: Rights and Wrongs.* Princeton, NJ: Princeton University Press, 2008.

Wood, W. Jay. "Prudence." In *Virtues and Their Vices*, edited by Kevin Timpe and Craig A. Boyd, 37–58. New York: Oxford University Press, 2014.

Worthington, Everett L. Jr., and Scott T. Allison. *Heroic Humility.* Washington, DC: American Psychological Association, 2018.

Worthington, Everett L. Jr., and Steven J. Sandage. *Forgiveness and Spirituality in Psychotherapy.* Washington, DC: American Psychological Association, 2016.

Zagzebski, Linda. "Trust." In *Virtues and Their Vices*, edited by Kevin Timpe and Craig A. Boyd, 269–84. New York: Oxford University Press, 2014.

CPSIA information can be obtained
at www.ICGtesting.com
Printed in the USA
BVHW031358150722
642230BV00013B/1195

9 781626 984288